Blessed be the name of our God; let us sing to his praise, yea, let us give thanks to his holy name, for he doth work righteousness forever...my joy is full, yea, my heart is brim with joy, and I will rejoice in my God.

Now the joy of Ammon was so great even that he was full; yea, he was swallowed up in the joy of his God...this is joy which none receiveth save it be the truly penitent and humble seeker of happiness.

—Alma 26:8, 11, 27:17-18

THE HUMBLE SEEKER OF
HAPPINESS

LESSONS IN JOY FROM THE BOOK OF MORMON

By Dane C. Hurst

Copyright © 2023 by Dane C. Hurst.

All rights reserved. No portion of this book may be reproduced in any form without written permission from the author, except as permitted by law.

ISBN: 9798218325787

This publication is designed to provide personal perspectives in regard to the subject matter. It is sold with the understanding that the author is not engaged in counseling, therapy, or other professional services. The views presented here are solely those of the author and do not necessarily represent the doctrines or positions of the Church of Jesus Christ of Latter-Day Saints.

Cover image stylized from Adobe Stock used under license.
Cover design and illustrations by Danielle R. Hurst

First edition 2023

www.humblyseeking.com

For my dad, Joe, who perpetuated a heritage of thoughtful writing

And for my eternal co-seeker, Danielle

Contents

Preface 1
    A Personal Connection and Invitation 5

The Humble Seeker of Happiness 9
    Ammon's Story 11
    Ammon's Reflection 20
        Truly Penitent 20
        Humble 22
        Seeker of Happiness 25
    Have We Not Reason to Rejoice? 32

Living After the Manner of Happiness 35
    Happiness and Mortality 38

This Vale of Sorrow 45
    Death and Wickedness 46
    Complex Feelings 48
    Antidotes for Sorrow 51
    Righteousness and Sorrow 53
    Evolution of Sorrow 57
        Negative Examples 58
        Positive Examples 59
    A Call to the Work is a Call to Mourn 63
    A Man of Sorrows 65

By Me Ye Are Led 69
    Lehites 70
    Jaredites 81
    Promise Lands 85
    Roadmap to Your Personal Promised Land 87
        Focus on Positivity 88
        Minister to Others 89
        Seek and Receive Personal Revelation 91
        Use Agency Righteously 95
        Wait on the Lord 98

THE PLAN OF HAPPINESS 105
    THE HAPPINESS PREPARED FOR THE SAINTS 106
    HOW GREAT IS THE PLAN! 111
    RESTORATION AND REDEMPTION 114
        Plan of Restoration 118
        Plan of Redemption 123

FRUIT TO MAKE ONE HAPPY 127
    SISTER TREES 130
    FRUIT AND HARVESTING 135
    WATER 138

POSTFACE 145
    ANOTHER INVITATION 147
    MY TRANSFORMATIVE EXPERIENCE 149
        Divine Happiness 149
        Scripture Study 150
        Coming unto Christ 152

APPENDIX A | CITATION INDEX 157
    BOOK OF MORMON 157
    OTHER SCRIPTURES 163
    GENERAL CONFERENCE 164
    MISCELLANEOUS 165

APPENDIX B | BOOK OF MORMON VERSE COUNT TIMELINE 167

PREFACE

This book was an accident.

The world is filled with secular and religious advice about happiness, and I am not especially qualified to add yet another voice to the cacophony. I am not a devout reader and have not aspired to write a book since I was eight years old. (Incidentally, that was about when my interest in recreational reading peaked.) I am college educated, but not in a field like English, psychology, or philosophy that would have prepared me for this task. I have not been the victim of significant discrimination, trauma, or tragedy, so I have neither the authority of notable lived experience nor an unusually exciting personal story to share. I am not always happy.

I am, however, a human. I have had ups, downs, and a lot of in-betweens. I try to make sense out of life each day, but most days feel unfruitful in that pursuit. In short, I am just a regular guy living a regular life and can easily blend into a crowd.

I am also a student of the scriptures. I love God's word, especially as it is recorded in the Book of Mormon.

I have often pondered the significance of the aphorism "the Book of Mormon was written for our day." I do not know that I am totally settled in my answer to that question, but in my pursuit of it, I have been led on a transformative study journey. For several years, I have found joy in studying the Book of Mormon in a way that "speaketh unto [me] according to [my] language, unto [my] understanding"[1]: spreadsheets. My personal studies have focused on turning the text of the Book of Mormon into a database that can be used to find patterns

---

[1] 2 Nephi 31:3

and make connections. With the tools I have created, I can create a list of verses based on a multi-layered word search,[2] generate a timeline showing the number of verses recorded in each year,[3] tell you which verse is the most dense in references to God,[4] and provide all sorts of other information of various degrees of value.[5]

As I was nearing the end of one such study project, I realized that I needed a change of pace to keep my interest level up, and that new pace needed to be something less technical. Recognizing the potential of the tools I had created, I started pondering how I could study the "written for our day" question in unique ways. I shortly arrived at the topic of happiness. It was a topic of personal importance that I also felt had great relevance to larger society. I concluded that I should study the topic of happiness in the Book of Mormon and write a Sacrament Meeting talk on the subject. I did not ever expect to deliver the talk, but it was a convenient tool to frame my thinking. I was motivated by a truth Sacrament Meeting speakers often discover: the power of the experience is in preparing—not delivering—the talk.

---

[2] There are eight verses that contain "happiness" and "misery" together. They are 2 Nephi 2:11, 2 Nephi 2:13, Alma 3:26, Alma 40:15, Alma 40:17, Alma 40:21, Alma 41:4, and Mormon 8:38.

[3] See Appendix B

[4] 3 Nephi 9:18 and 3 Nephi 11:7 each have six names or pronouns for Heavenly Father or Jesus Christ and twenty total words. Moroni 4:3 (Moroni's version of the blessing on the sacramental bread) has the most total references to God, at 18 references in 91 words.

[5] There are 268,638 words in the English edition of the Book of Mormon when you count Mormon's original writings that are not assigned verse numbers (such as the title page and book headings). The middle two words are "boast of" in Alma 26:12. The rest of that verse is "Yea, I know that I am nothing; as to my strength I am weak; therefore I will not boast of myself, but I will boast of my God, for in his strength I can do all things; yea, behold, many mighty miracles we have wrought in this land, for which we will praise his name forever." Thus, the literal central message of the Book of Mormon is Ammon's declaration of humility, proclamation of faith, and praise for God's miracles. Take that all for what it is worth.

As I began an intentional study on this topic, my mind and spirit exploded with understanding. Stories and doctrines that I had read, studied, and taught dozens of times previously came alive in vibrant color as I looked at them through this new lens. I made connections that seemed so obvious that I marveled at how I could have ever missed them. Sometimes, the things I was learning were so beautiful that I "felt to sing the song of redeeming love"[6] and the best expression of my feelings was to rehearse in my mind lines of sacred hymns such as, "I stand all amazed!"[7] and "How great Thou art!"[8]

Studying the story of Lehi eating from the Tree of Life became increasingly relatable. I was filled with so much joy in tasting the fruit of the love of God that I instinctively, impulsively, wanted to share it with others. I also realized the volume of content I was discovering was far greater than anything that could be delivered in a Sacrament Meeting talk, so I started thinking bigger. I decided to instead write a book, still without the expectation that it would be published, but with the understanding that the value of the experience would be in organizing my thoughts on paper.

I tell the backstory of this book to reveal my own bias and underscore my intentions. Though I am not an expert in psychology or theology, I can say with certainty that the Spirit of God has led my studying and writing. In saying that, I recognize it was personal revelation and not necessarily directly applicable to anyone else. This is not a pronouncement of doctrine of the Church of Jesus Christ of Latter-Day Saints. This is not a commentary on clinical depression, anxiety, or any other mental illness or emotional condition. This is nothing more than a record of one man's understanding of the scriptures applied to

---

[6] Alma 5:26

[7] "I Stand All Amazed", *Hymns of the Church of Jesus Christ of Latter-Day Saints.* Deseret Book Company, Salt Lake City, Utah. 1985.

[8] "How Great Thou Art", *Hymns of the Church of Jesus Christ of Latter-Day Saints.* Deseret Book Company, Salt Lake City, Utah. 1985.

the topic of happiness. It is written from the perspective of someone navigating universal, everyday challenges and trials.

The subject of happiness is universally relevant but intensely personal in its application. Knowing my own limitations, I have been deliberate in documenting the scriptural backing for my assertions and intentional in keeping my own experiences at a distance. Anyone else with a different life experience will interpret the same passages differently and be inspired with their own action items from them. My task has simply been to comment on scriptural teachings on the subject. I have faith that the Spirit will touch you with an individualized understanding of what it all means for you personally.

Though this book is outwardly about happiness, increased joy is at best the third most important lesson I hope you will take from it. In a reverent way, my foremost hope is that this book will serve the same purpose as its primary reference, which is to be yet another testament of Jesus Christ. At its core, this book is about understanding the personal nature of Christ's atoning sacrifice, discovering your unique role in God's Plan of Happiness, and being motivated to accept the grace of Christ as you work towards the ultimate gift God has in store for you: to join with Him in experiencing eternal joy.

The second most important lesson from this book is a testament of the power of scripture study. These writings are personal and sacred to me because of the many experiences I have had communicating with the Spirit in writing them. They will not have the same powerful effect on anyone else who superficially reads them. I hope that reading this book will motivate you to deepen your relationship with God's word.

This book is not meant to be read cover to cover and then set back on the shelf. Each chapter (and most sections within each chapter) can stand independently. My encouragement to you is to use the Table of Contents and Citation Index to find a topic of interest and jump straight to it. Please study the cited scriptural passages and consider the doctrines and stories in their full context. Most importantly, I pray you will be inspired to search the scriptures, words of latter-day prophets, and your own life experiences for your own answers. Make your own connections.[9] Take notes in the margins or a study journal. When you are done studying happiness, put this book down (even if you have not read it completely) and start studying another subject that speaks to you in a way that makes sense to you.

A Personal Connection and Invitation

Professionally, I am an airport engineering consultant. When the owner of an airport (such as a city government) wants to improve their infrastructure (like upgrading a runway or expanding a parking apron) they will often hire a company like mine to act as agents on their behalf to oversee the successful completion of that project. To fulfill that role, my colleagues and I interpret the relevant standards of the Federal Aviation Administration (FAA) and other agencies, collect pertinent data, and then apply the standards to the project-specific constraints to develop a design. Typically, we prepare construction drawings, technical specifications, and other contract documents and then ask for bids from interested contractors to physically complete the work.

As engineers, we are careful to focus on the "what" of the project and to leave the "how" to the contractors who complete the construction. When a contractor wants to build one of our projects, they submit a bid by giving us a formal cost proposal, together with preliminary evidence that they understand the project requirements and can complete the work.

---

[9] I know for certain that there are many more connections that could be made than those I have referenced in this text. I have intentionally focused on the Book of Mormon, but much could be added to what I have written by referencing the stories and doctrines in other scriptures. Much has been spoken (and much more will be spoken) in General Conference about the topics I have addressed, but I have made only light references to the teachings of Church leaders. My hope is that this approach will maximize the space for your own connections to be made.

After we have awarded the project to the successful bidder (but before we authorize the work to begin) the contractor must provide detailed evidence that they can meet the standards we have outlined in the contract documents. Depending on the complexity of the project, this can be a painstaking process and result in a mountain of paperwork. For example, the contractor needs to prove that the materials that will be delivered (gravel, asphalt, pipes, etc.) will meet strict FAA specifications. They must also provide proof of insurance, project schedules, materials testing plans, safety plans—the list could go on.

As a rule, the standards that govern airport construction are more stringent than for most other types of infrastructure. That is because things happen at airports—fast, heavy things—that do not happen anywhere else. Sometimes, a contractor will remind us that our project requirements are not typical for other projects they normally work on, and then ask for leniency. But as engineers who "protect and advance the health, safety, and welfare"[10] of the flying public and represent the interests of our clients, we cannot yield on the requirements that were established in the original contract documents. A contractor chooses to accept the standards of the project when they submit a bid proposal. After the contract is signed, the contractor is legally bound first to demonstrate how they will ensure those standards are met, and secondly deliver on their commitments.

Though I am not trained in the humanities, my professional training is more applicable to writing this book than what it seems on the surface. I used the same approach in writing this book that I use when developing the design of an airfield construction project. I sought to understand applicable standards, collected data, analyzed patterns, made judgements on how to apply the standards, and then communicated my thoughts to others and will allow them the liberty to make practical use of my design.

---

[10] American Society of Civil Engineers (ASCE) Code of Ethics. Updated October 26, 2020.

To paraphrase a term from my professional work, I invite you to prepare a "Plan of Happiness Compliance Document (PHCD)"[11] as you study. In other words, take some time to document specifically how you will live God's laws and be qualified for His eternal blessings. You accepted His standards when you fought in premortality to come to earth. You were awarded a figurative contract when you entered the waters of baptism. It is now your obligation to fulfill your covenants in faith and patience. A personal PHCD, developed in conjunction with the Spirit, will become a trusted guide to your discipleship and a sacred treasure.

God has full faith in your ability to be successful. His standards are high and unyielding because his rewards are not found anywhere else. His standards are universal, but your path to eternal happiness will be personal. You cannot find it explicitly written in the words of this or any other book, post, or article. But as you immerse yourself in God's word and strive for communion with the Spirit, your path will be revealed to you; and it will be "wonderful, wonderful to [you]!"[12]

---

[11] My professional life is so saturated with complex jargon, I could not resist adding to the heap. The original term is "Safety Plan Compliance Document (SPCD)." It is a document that an airfield contractor must submit prior to construction to certify that they understand the safety requirements of the project and outline specific actions they will take to meet them.

[12] "I Stand All Amazed", *Hymns of the Church of Jesus Christ of Latter-Day Saints.* Deseret Book Company, Salt Lake City, Utah. 1985.

The Humble Seeker of Happiness

The most colorful illustration of joy in the Book of Mormon is Ammon, the son of King Mosiah. On one occasion, his expressions of joy were so effusive that he drew criticism from his brother.[1] At least two other times, he experienced such intense joy that he lost his strength and became physically incapacitated for a time.[2]

Most of us are familiar with various degrees of happiness, but few have ever felt such immense joy as to be overwhelmed into unconsciousness. Even if that incapacitating kind of joy may not be our goal, many of us have a perpetual, innate human desire to have more meaningful and more regular experiences with joy. The scriptures, being a divinely gifted guidebook for mortality, are filled with teachings on this subject. With Ammon being a quintessential example of joy, a study of his life and ministry is highly informative to our efforts to find divine, inexpressible joy.

Joy is not an accidental lesson from Ammon's story. The scriptural writers intentionally taught about his experiences with joy for our benefit in the latter days. When Mormon abridged the Large Plates of Nephi, he recounted one of Ammon's episodes of fainting from joy and then made the editorial comment that, "this is joy which none receiveth save it be the *truly penitent and humble seeker of happiness.*"[3]

---

[1] See Alma 26:10
[2] See Alma 19:14, 27:17; In writing this chapter, I lightheartedly nicknamed Ammon "Joy Boy" because of his penchant for over-the-top experiences with happiness. Just imagine the fun his brothers might have had with him being the guest of honor at a surprise party!
[3] Alma 27:18, emphasis added.

The word "penitent" in this description is especially provocative. Noah Webster's 1828 *American Dictionary of the English Language*[4] defines "penitent" as:

> *"Suffering pain or sorrow of heart on account of sins, crimes or offences; contrite; sincerely affected by a sense of guilt and resolving on amendment of life."*[5]

Expanding this definition, the same reference describes being "contrite" as:

> *"Literally, worn or bruised. Hence, broken-hearted for sin; deeply affected with grief and sorrow for having offended God."*[6]

And "amendment" means:

> *"An alteration or change for the better; correction of a fault or faults; reformation of life, by quitting vices."*[7]

In an over-simplified conclusion, Ammon's story teaches us that seeking happiness is not for the faint of heart (though fainting is a part of his story). Ammon experienced overpowering joy only because he had suffered pain and a sorrowful heart. He had been worn, bruised, and

---

[4] Noah Webster's 1828 *American Dictionary of the English Language* is a valuable tool in understanding the Book of Mormon. Not only is it the earliest comprehensive dictionary of American English, but it was published while the Book of Mormon was being translated. Because of that, it gives an excellent window into Joseph Smith's understanding of the English language as he sought for words to record as a translation of the golden plates.

[5] "Penitent", American Dictionary of the English Language. Noah Webster, 14 April 1828.

[6] "Contrite", American Dictionary of the English Language. Noah Webster, 14 April 1828.

[7] "Amendment", American Dictionary of the English Language. Noah Webster, 14 April 1828.

broken hearted.[8] But he did not stand by and wait for happiness to happen to him, feeling entitled to joy simply because he had known misery. His guilt led him to a "reformation of life," and he actively searched for divine happiness.

Consider Mormon's statement about Ammon and these definitions as we review his life story, as recorded in the Book of Mormon. There is ample evidence that Ammon's life experiences qualified him as a "truly penitent and humble seeker of happiness" and was thus deserving of the joy he experienced.

Ammon's Story

Ammon was born into royalty as one of at least four sons of King Mosiah and a grandson of King Benjamin. We do not know anything about his mother or grandmother, but we know enough of his father and grandfather to be assured that he was raised in a righteous, well-grounded environment. Ammon was part of a generation, though, that openly questioned and fought against the doctrines and practices taught by their parents. They, and he, used overt deception and flattery to destroy the Church of God.[9] One of their chief comrades in this effort was Alma, the son of Alma who was the leader of the Church. When studying the scriptural account of the worry that the senior Alma and King Mosiah had over the wickedness of the rising generation, it is important to remember that their concerns would have been very personal in nature.[10]

For this group of rebellious young men, the day of reckoning came in a dramatic fashion. As they went about their seditious work, an angel of the Lord appeared to them in a cloud and called them to repentance with a thunderous, ground-shaking voice. They were so astonished that they fell to the ground. This portion of the record focuses on Alma's

---

[8] See Alma 17:5
[9] See Mosiah 26:1-7 and 27:8, 10
[10] See Mosiah 26:8-13 and 27:1-5

experience, who was in an incapacitated state for two full days. He was not just passively laying there but was being made acutely aware of the awful state of his soul and the glorious redemption of Christ.[11] When he arose, he recounted his experience with the opening statement, "I have repented of my sins, and have been redeemed of the Lord; behold I am born of the Spirit".[12]

Though the record focuses on Alma, it can be assumed that the sons of Mosiah and others with them had a similar experience. Regardless of the specifics of what they each saw, heard, and felt, we know that Ammon and the others "began from this time forward to teach the people…publishing to all the people the things which they had heard and seen, and preaching the word of God in much tribulation, being greatly persecuted by those who were unbelievers, being smitten by many of them. But notwithstanding all this, they did impart much consolation to the church, confirming their faith, and exhorting them with long-suffering and much travail to keep the commandments of God."[13]

They began their ministering efforts locally, striving to repair the destruction they had previously caused among the church,[14] but soon grew loftier ambitions. The sons of Mosiah approached their dad—the king—to seek permission to preach among the Lamanites. Their goal was to cure centuries-old prejudices between these two societies. Their own experience with redemption from being "the very vilest of sinners" was so fresh, that their desires to prevent similar "anguish of soul"[15] in any other human cut through every prejudice they might have held. They received permission to take this missionary journey only after their father received divine confirmation through revelation and the assurance that they would be delivered by the hand of the Lord.[16]

---

[11] See Mosiah 27:11-23
[12] Mosiah 27:24 (24-31)
[13] Mosiah 27:32-33
[14] See Mosiah 27:32-37
[15] Mosiah 28:4
[16] See Mosiah 28:1-8

The weight of the unknown would have increased in every footstep closer to the Lamanites on their multi-day journey. Though they were undoubtedly excited for the impending adventure, they were also not ignorant of the personal safety risks they were imposing on themselves. As they traveled, they fasted and prayed for the Lord to attend them, and He did. Not only did He speak comfort to them, but He counseled them to be patient in their suffering and promised success in their efforts.[17]

Ammon was the leader of this group of missionaries. When they got to the borders of the land, they paused long enough for Ammon to administer a priesthood blessing to each one. Then each young man went his own way, relying entirely on the Spirit to direct his individual travels and ministering efforts. They could do no more than to trust in the promises of the Lord that they would one day meet again having had remarkable success.[18]

Ammon was led by the Spirit to a part of the Lamanite territory called Ishmael. Upon setting foot into his mission area, Ammon was at once arrested and taken before the king of Ishmael, named Lamoni. Ammon's likely prospects at that point were to be killed, made a slave, cast into prison, or be expelled from the land. When Ammon expressed a desire to stay in Ishmael on a long-term basis, even offering himself as a servant to the king, it impressed Lamoni very much. Not only did Lamoni forebear from any of the cruel punishments Ammon might have expected, but he offered one of his daughters in marriage, which Ammon refused.[19]

One of his first duties as a servant of the king was to help take the king's flocks to a communal watering hole. While there, thieves tried to steal the animals, as they had done many times previously. While his fellow servants wept for fear of being slain (whether by the thieves or by a displeased king, we cannot be sure), Ammon saw an opportunity to

---

[17] See Alma 17:9-12
[18] See Alma 17:13-18
[19] See Alma 17:20-25

win the hearts of his fellow servants, whom he considered to be brothers. Coupled with encouragement to be cheerful, Ammon urged them to action in defending the flocks and their own lives. They did so successfully.[20]

After returning to the king's court, the other servants marveled to Lamoni about what they had experienced. The power that Ammon had displayed left such an impression on them that they supposed he may have been God in the flesh. The mystery surrounding Ammon's greatness multiplied when it was discovered that he was fulfilling his menial duties, even as everyone else was caught up in the excitement of the day. King Lamoni's awe for Ammon deepened to the point that he was nervous to even ask him into his presence.[21] When Lamoni found the courage to do so—and of course, Ammon willingly came—he was speechless. He did not even know where to begin. Being "wise yet harmless"[22], Ammon recognized an opportunity and taught a wide-ranging gospel lesson to the king. Ammon's teaching had such a powerful effect as to cause Lamoni to fall to the ground in such a way that some thought he was dead for two days.[23]

Despite the confusion among the king's family and servants, Ammon had an intimate understanding of the state Lamoni was in during this period. "He *knew* that king Lamoni was under the power of God." "He *knew* that the dark veil of unbelief was being cast away from his mind." He *knew* "the light which did light up his mind, which was the light of the glory of God." He knew all these things by experience—Ammon had a remarkably similar conversion experience within recent memory. "This light had infused such joy into *his* soul, the cloud of darkness having been dispelled [so that] the light of everlasting life was lit up in *his* soul." He *knew* that this kind of exposure to the Spirit of God could be so powerful as to "overcome his natural frame, and [be] carried away in

---

[20] See Alma 17:26-39
[21] See Alma 18:2-11
[22] Alma 18:22 (12-23)
[23] See Alma 18:24-43 and 19:1-5

God."²⁴ While others looked upon Lamoni's incapacitation with fear and mourning, Ammon looked upon him with understanding and joyful anticipation.

The following day, Lamoni awoke from his three-day-long experience with the Spirit of the Lord to find his wife faithfully watching at his bedside. His heart overflowed with gratitude as he praised her and God. He testified and prophesied of *his* Redeemer. This new testimony filled his soul with joy. The queen likewise experienced joy as a response to her husband's testimony, even though she had not yet had a profound conversion. Their collective joy was so great that they were both overcome by the Spirit and fell to the ground.²⁵

Ammon watched these events with complete wonderment. In this moment, he recognized that his prayers for success were being answered in an unfathomable way and fell to his knees in prayer and thanksgiving. While in this attitude of praise, he was overpowered with joy to the point of being incapacitated.²⁶

Ammon arose from his trip into unconsciousness to a scene of great commotion. However, he found the king and queen joyfully teaching and testifying of Christ and the truths Ammon had taught them.²⁷ Lamoni's servants later joined in testifying of their own conversion experience. In turn, their testimonies helped persuade other people to be baptized. Surely, Ammon had great reason to be astonished.²⁸

Having proven himself well among Lamoni's people, Ammon's thoughts turned to his companions elsewhere among the Lamanites. Specifically, he received revelation that his brother Aaron and two others were in prison in Middoni. He was impressed that he needed to go liberate them, so he set out to do so with Lamoni as his companion.²⁹

---

[24] Alma 19:6, emphasis added.
[25] See Alma 19:11-13
[26] See Alma 19:14
[27] See Alma 19:28-33
[28] See Alma 19:33-36
[29] See Alma 20:1-7

Along the way, they encountered Lamoni's father—the king of all Lamanites. He was exceptionally displeased with his son and Ammon was at the center of the dispute. The king threatened Ammon's life, then turned his ire towards Lamoni. Ammon interceded with his "wise [and bold] yet harmless"[30] manner and was able to not only quench the violent rhetoric, but to convince the king to liberate Ammon's brethren and grant Lamoni greater sovereignty.[31] Incidentally, the king also developed a desire to be taught the gospel. He was convinced of all these things primarily because he recognized the love that Ammon had for Lamoni.[32]

Ammon and Lamoni continued their journey and successfully freed Aaron, Muloki and Ammah from prison. The experiences of these three missionaries were vastly different than Ammon's improbable acceptance and success among Lamoni's people. These three companions of Ammon had been rejected, cast out, smitten, driven from place to place, and then imprisoned. When Ammon found them, they were naked, hungry, thirsty and had worn skin from being tied up. They had been patient through these afflictions, but seeing their desperate situation caused deep sorrow within Ammon.[33] It is easy to imagine Ammon feeling a mix of guilt and gratitude in recognizing how easily he could have suffered the same fate.[34]

Afterward, Ammon and Lamoni returned to the land of *their* inheritance in Ishmael, where Lamoni's respect for his friend was evident in refusing to let Ammon serve him.[35] Instead, Ammon was witness to the people being granted religious and other liberties. He saw

---

[30] Alma 18:22
[31] See Alma 20:8-27; Consider the range of emotions Ammon must have felt standing there as his friend's own father threatened to kill him (after failing in his encouragement for Lamoni to kill Ammon), all because of the changes Ammon had elicited in Lamoni.
[32] See Alma 22:3
[33] See Alma 20:28-30
[34] See Alma 17:20
[35] See Alma 21:18-19

synagogues being built. Ammon had free reign to preach the gospel daily and the people were "zealous" in their response.[36] This would have been a golden age for Ammon—something he could not have fantasized when he started his missionary service.

While Ammon and Lamoni were facilitating this remarkable transformation in Ishmael, Aaron and his companions were led by the Spirit to the land of Nephi. This was the home of Lamoni's father, the king of all Lamanites *except* Lamoni's people. Through their ministry to him, Lamoni's father was likewise converted to the gospel.[37] His conversion marked the beginning of an important new era for all Lamanite civilization, and Ammon would not have been ignorant of his direct role in making this happen. Ammon and all his companions had total liberty to preach the gospel in any Lamanite territory. Beyond the religious implications of this liberty, it signaled significant cultural, social, and economic improvements first for the Lamanites and then the Nephites.[38]

However, not everything associated with this transformation was positive. In the face of these remarkable changes, Ammon saw a growing hostility towards his adopted brethren, to the point that civil war became a real possibility. Never being one to stand idly by, Ammon gathered his brethren and held a council about how to respond to these threats.[39]

When the threats of violence materialized, the converted Lamanites (now known as the people of Anti-Nephi-Lehi) willingly subjected themselves to the swords of their fellow Lamanites, rather than engaging in bloodshed themselves. Hundreds were killed in a prone

---

[36] See Alma 21:23 (20-23)

[37] See Alma 22:1 (1-25)

[38] See Alma 22:25-27 and 23:1-6, 18

[39] Alma 24:1-5; As with Ammon's first encounter with Lamoni's father, one must wonder about Ammon's emotional response to seeing violence arise as a side effect of the changes he had introduced to the Lamanites (see Alma 20:8-16).

position. However, a thousand of their assailants were moved with compassion and were converted. This would have been a highly emotional experience for anyone watching, including Ammon.[40]

For some Lamanites, this violence fueled an increased thirst for bloodshed, and they turned their vengeance toward the Nephites and many more battles came out of that contrived conflict.[41] However, the Lamanites were not successful in their bid to overpower the Nephites. As a result, even more Lamanites were humbled and joined the people of Anti-Nephi-Lehi in their covenant of peace.[42] Unfortunately, though, the repeated military disappointments further angered another subgroup of the Lamanites, the Amalekites, so they came back yet again to destroy the people of Anti-Nephi-Lehi. If subjugation is what they looked for, they found a remarkably easy target with these people. Their commitment to their covenants once again led them to refuse to defend themselves against an unprovoked attack.[43]

Ammon and his brethren knew that this "great work of destruction" was not a sustainable course for these people with whom there was mutual profound love. They knew that the people would have hope of refuge only if they lived in the shadow of Zarahemla. When they offered this solution to the king, he recognized some obvious complications, namely that the Nephites and Lamanites had historically had a difficult relationship. The king knew the Nephites had little reason to trust or offer mercy to his people. The king agreed to the plan only after Ammon had sought for (and received) confirmation through revelation that this course of action was divinely approved. And so, the people once again showed remarkable faith by gathering their possessions and traveling towards Zarahemla with only a hope that they would be received as refugees among the Nephites.[44]

---

[40] See Alma 24:6-27
[41] See Alma 25:1-3
[42] See Alma 25:13-14
[43] See Alma 27:1-3
[44] See Alma 27:4-14

On the outskirts of Zarahemla, the people stopped while the Nephite missionaries went all the way into the Nephite capital to discover the attitude of the people concerning this group of refugees. It was on this last leg of the journey that the missionaries met up again with their old friend Alma, following a fourteen-year absence.[45] In response to this reunion, it was noted, "Now the joy of Ammon was so great even that he was full; yea, he was swallowed up in the joy of his God, even to the exhausting of his strength; and he fell again to the earth."[46] These were the events that elicited Mormon's observation that "this is joy which none receiveth save it be the *truly penitent and humble seeker of happiness*".[47] Everyone involved had "truly great" joy, but it was Ammon who stole the show with his physical reaction.[48]

The people of Anti-Nephi-Lehi were eagerly received by the Nephites and went on to shape Nephite culture and history in meaningful ways. At the time of their assimilation into Nephite society, this group became known as the people of Ammon, as a lasting testament of the role he played in their story.[49]

Several years later, the military captain Moroni became a central figure in Nephite history and a revered hero of the Book of Mormon. He was described as, "A strong and a mighty man; he was a man of a perfect understanding...a man whose heart did swell with thanksgiving to his God, for the many privileges and blessings which he bestowed upon his people; a man who did labor exceedingly for the welfare and safety of his people. Yea, and he was a man who was firm in the faith of Christ".[50] The quality of Moroni's character was further underscored by the reflection, "If all men had been, and were, and ever would be, like unto Moroni, behold, the very powers of hell would have been shaken

---

[45] See Alma 27:16 and Alma 17:1-4
[46] Alma 27:17
[47] Alma 27:18, emphasis added.
[48] Alma 27:19
[49] See Alma 27:26 (20-30)
[50] Alma 48:11-13

forever; yea, the devil would never have power over the hearts of the children of men." If the writer had not yet adequately described Moroni's nature, he felt to add one last qualifying statement, "He was a man like unto Ammon...[a man] of God".[51] In other words, not only do the praises for Moroni apply to Ammon (and his brethren) but he (and they) was an archetype to describe the character of Moroni.[52]

Ammon's Reflection

Nestled in the historical record between the second wave of defenseless attacks from the Amalekites (with its consequent wave of conversions) and the exodus of the people of Anti-Nephi-Lehi to Zarahemla, we find an extended account of the rejoicings of Ammon and his brothers concerning all they had seen and experienced.[53]

In this reflection, we learn directly from Ammon how he exemplified each part of the description of a "truly penitent and humble seeker of happiness."[54] As you study these qualifications, consider the role each of them plays in your own search for happiness.

Truly Penitent

As discussed previously, penitence is all about repentance. It is a recognition of one's guilt and subsequent efforts to improve behaviors. In the context of the gospel of Jesus Christ, penitence invokes the idea of "godly sorrow"[55] as a disciple exercises faith to transform from a natural man into saint through the atonement of Jesus Christ.[56]

---

[51] Alma 48:17-18
[52] See Alma 49:30 and Ether 12:15 for more examples of Ammon's long-lasting legacy.
[53] See Alma 25:17 and 26:1-37
[54] Alma 27:18
[55] See 2 Corinthians 7:10, James 4:8-10, Alma 36: 12-14 (6-28), Alma 42:29, and Moroni 2:13
[56] See Mosiah 3:19

The sons of Mosiah had once been in an "awful, sinful, and polluted state"[57]. They earned a designation as the "very vilest of sinners"[58] as they rebelliously tried to destroy the faith and discipleship of others, and thus hinder the work of the church of God.[59] But in the infinite mercy of God,[60] they were offered a chance to repent, which they accepted whole-heartedly. They felt the weighty guilt of their sins, but they committed the rest of their lives to the service of God to repair the damages they caused. Their motivation was to allow other sinners to experience the same redemptive healing they had found. Their faith was greater than their fear of ridicule or physical danger. Their hearts were changed forever.[61]

Ammon promised that the change of heart he experienced is available to anyone who will repent, exercise faith in Christ, do good works, and pray continually. As you do so, you are promised you will come to understand the mysteries of God.[62] On one level, that promise may be thought of as a divine search engine where we ask questions and God reveals the answers. Questions about understanding doctrines and seeking guidance for personal decisions are valid and proper to ask. Penitence will enhance your sensitivity to the Spirt and ability to receive personal revelation. However, Ammon's experience and testimony point to an even more significant variety of mysteries that only the penitent can understand.

The greatest of all mysteries is that Christ and Heavenly Father know each of us intimately (including our weaknesses, faults, and insecurities), yet they continually plead with each of us to use their healing, redeeming, and enabling power to become perfected as they are. As you faithfully accept them, you will develop the same knowledge,

---

[57] Alma 26:17
[58] Mosiah 28:4
[59] See Mosiah 27:8-10
[60] Alma 26:17-20
[61] See Mosiah 5:2 (2-8)
[62] See Alma 26:21-22

understanding, and happiness that Ammon had when he bore his witness. That is not only the greatest mystery, but also the greatest gift that any of us could pursue.

HUMBLE

Ammon described their group of missionaries as "instruments in the hands of God" in helping the Lamanites "behold the marvelous light of God".[63] In modern language, an "instrument" is understood as a specialized tool in fields like science and music that help a user discover the natural world or offer creative expression of unspoken thoughts and feelings. By themselves, these devices would be lifeless and never achieve the good they were created to do. Their value is only realized when in the hands of a master user. However, the most skilled scientist or musician is helpless without the tools necessary to practice their craft. When an instrument is taken up in the hands of a master, it becomes an extension of their person and is how their knowledge, intuition and objectives are made manifest.[64] "Shall the axe boast itself against him that heweth therewith? Or shall the saw magnify itself against him that shaketh it?"[65] No. A tool is no better than the person using it.

This group of missionaries started their journey with a prayer that they would be instruments in God's hands. In return, the Lord commanded them to be comforted, to be patient in suffering and to be

---

[63] Alma 26:3

[64] This metaphor is particularly intriguing when considering scientific instruments, like a telescope, which help their user discover physical light in the universe God created, just as the missionaries had been "instruments in the hands of God" to help the Lamanites "behold the marvelous light of God." See Alma 19:6 for added insight on the link between divine light and joy.

[65] Isaiah 10:15

good examples of Him.[66] They did those things, so the Lord fulfilled His promise and answered their prayer.[67]

Describing himself as an instrument in God's hands was a tremendous act of humility for Ammon. He had offered himself a willing servant to King Lamoni. He had fought off the band of robbers. He had impressed the king with his diligence and wisdom. He had taught the gospel to the king, queen, and all their household. He had delivered his brothers from prison and in the process, he softened the heart of Lamoni's father, and elicited drastic social and political changes throughout all Lamanite territories. He made it possible for thousands of Lamanites to know the Lord. But none of these things were about Ammon. They were about Ammon doing God's work by God's power. All glory, praise, and honor for these miraculous events went to Him. Ammon told his brothers:

> *I do not boast in my own strength, nor in my own wisdom; but behold, my joy is full, yea, my heart is brim with joy, and I will rejoice in my God.*
>
> *Yea, I know that I am nothing; as to my strength I am weak; therefore I will not boast of myself, but I will boast of my God, for in his strength I can do all things; yea, behold, many mighty miracles we have wrought in this land, for which we will praise his name forever.*
>
> *Behold, how many thousands of our brethren has he loosed from the pains of hell; and they are brought to sing redeeming love, and this because of the power of his word which is in us, therefore have we not great reason to rejoice?*

---

[66] See Alma 17:9-11
[67] See Alma 25:17

> *Yea, we have reason to praise him forever, for he is the Most High God, and has loosed our brethren from the chains of hell.*
>
> *Yea, they were encircled about with everlasting darkness and destruction; but behold, he has brought them into his everlasting light, yea, into everlasting salvation; and they are encircled about with the matchless bounty of his love; yea, and we have been instruments in his hands of doing this great and marvelous work.*
>
> *Therefore, let us glory, yea, we will glory in the Lord; yea, we will rejoice, for our joy is full; yea, we will praise our God forever. Behold, who can glory too much in the Lord? Yea, who can say too much of his great power, and of his mercy, and of his long-suffering towards the children of men? Behold, I say unto you, I cannot say the smallest part which I feel.*[68]

As powerful as Ammon's words may be, they felt inadequate to fully convey his feelings of praise to God. He was experiencing an all-consuming wonder of God's power and mercy that was difficult to describe with mortal words. This profound joy only came because Ammon humbly acknowledged that any of his good works—especially bringing about the redemption of others—were possible only by yielding his understanding and efforts to He who is all-knowing and all-powerful.

The promise of joy springing from true humility is not isolated to Ammon. Jacob taught that the gate keeper on the straight and narrow path is the Holy One of Israel. He will open the gate for anyone who knocks, but anyone who comes in pride (because of their wealth and own wisdom) will be despised and not allowed to enter. Those who

---

[68] Alma 26:11-16

approach the gate in deep humility, considering themselves "fools before God" will be allowed to enter. These are they who qualify to receive the "things of the wise and the prudent," which is the "happiness which is prepared for the saints."[69]

In 41 B.C. the Nephites were riding a wave of prosperity in the church, joy, and peace. As predicted by the pride cycle, this prosperity led to pride in the hearts of some "who professed to belong to the church of God." That pride manifested itself as persecution of their humble fellow-members of the church. This group of humble believers responded with increased fasting and prayer. Consequently, they grew "*stronger* in their humility" and "*firmer* in the faith of Christ." Their example shows how humility is a precursor for joy, solace, and peace in the face of adversity. However, joy and peace were not the most significant blessing from their humility. They were simply indications of the grander blessing of their hearts being sanctified by Christ. That purification came because of "yielding (or giving way to) their hearts unto God."[70]

SEEKER OF HAPPINESS

Early in the missionaries' journey, even before they had found any Lamanites to minister to, the weight of the task they had nobly sought after was nearly unbearable.[71] Ammon described their depressed hearts and desires to turn back towards the comforts of home. As they debated their options, the Lord spoke to them and confirmed that they would not be excused from bearing afflictions, but also promised success in their labors. This promise was the comfort they needed to muster the courage to fulfill their mission. In time, both parts of the Lord's promises were fulfilled: they suffered many things but also found many successes. Their success only came because they diligently labored through

---

[69] 2 Nephi 9:41-43
[70] Helaman 3:35 (33-35) ; see also Moroni 10:32-33
[71] See Alma 17:7-12

adversity, trusting in the promises of the Lord.[72] Because of their diligent, deliberate seeking, they found immense joy.[73]

The scriptures have many forms of counsel around the topic of seeking. Whether the topic is serving in God's kingdom, a remission of sins, understanding the mysteries of God, or developing gifts of the Spirit, any lesson on seeking a divine gift is informative in our pursuit of any other. Consider how these examples of teachings related to seeking may apply specifically to your personal pursuit of happiness.

Serving in God's Kingdom

The inaugural First Presidency of the Church was organized in Kirtland, Ohio in March 1833. In preparation for that event, Joseph Smith received a revelation from the Lord that included counsel for several individuals related to their duties. In this context, the Lord gave the counsel and promise, "search diligently, pray always, and be believing, and all things shall work together for your good".[74] Nineteen months previous to that revelation, the Lord promised the saints in Zion, "he who doeth the works of righteousness shall receive…peace in this world, and eternal life in the world to come."[75]

In the Sermon on the Mount in Galilee, the Savior encouraged his disciples to seek "first the kingdom of God, and his righteousness; and all these things (namely, food, drink, and clothing) shall be added unto you."[76] This admonition expounds on teachings from earlier in the same sermon, when the Savior taught that earthly treasures are susceptible to degradation, corrosion, and theft. Heavenly treasures are not prone to corruption, so it is better to spend our energy in pursuit of them. The

---

[72] See Alma 26:27-30
[73] See Alma 26:35-37
[74] Doctrine and Covenants 90:24 (22-24)
[75] Doctrine and Covenants 59:23
[76] Matthew 6:33 (31-34)

Savior then taught that whatever our treasures may be, our hearts will be with them.[77]

To make this concept a little less abstract, the Savior also taught how we can measure where our hearts are at, and thus reveal the things we treasure most: The treasure of one's heart is reflected in the things that come out of his mouth.[78]

Taking these teachings together and applying them to the subject of happiness, we can conclude that happiness flows naturally out of a happy heart and a happy heart is one that has sought incorruptible heavenly treasures. Heavenly treasures are those things which serve to build up the kingdom of God.

Receiving a Remission of Sin

In 124 B.C., King Benjamin reminded his people of the importance of being wise and diligent in their efforts to "win the prize". There is room for broad application of this counsel but in context, the prize to which Benjamin referred was a daily remission of sin and being guiltless before God.[79] It is one matter to receive an initial forgiveness of sins, but the perpetual remission of sin requires consecrated seeking over a lifetime of discipleship.

We receive a remission of sin when we are baptized by water and receive the gift of the Holy Ghost.[80] We prove our commitment to keeping our baptismal covenants, and thus receive a continual remission of sin, by regularly and thoughtfully partaking of the sacrament.[81] In our daily living, we are bound to make mistakes and encounter other trials that require the healing power of the atonement of Jesus Christ. We come back to our baptismal covenants in a recurring way so that we can regularly receive that cleansing and mending of our souls. Ideally,

---

[77] See Matthew 6:19-21 and Luke 12:29-34
[78] See Luke 6:45 (43-45)
[79] See Mosiah 4:26-27
[80] See 2 Nephi 31:17
[81] See Doctrine and Covenants 20:77, 79

though, it is a cycle that moves upward like a spiral staircase. Each rotation through the process of cleansing, living life, sin, faith, and repentance should lead us closer to heaven.

The scriptures are full of teachings that relate forgiveness of sin to diligent effort. "He that repents and *does the commandments* of the Lord shall be forgiven."[82] The Savior's oft repeated plea to "*come* unto me"[83] implies movement on our part. Enos had to wrestle with God before he received a remission of sins.[84] Amulek implored the people on the hill Onidah to "begin to *exercise your faith* unto repentance, that ye begin to call upon his holy name, that he would have mercy upon you."[85] The pattern that Moroni followed for ordinations to the offices of the Aaronic Priesthood included an admonition to "preach repentance and remission of sins through Jesus Christ, by the *endurance of faith* on his name."[86]

When King Benjamin taught his people about winning "the prize," they had just had a remarkable conversion experience where they were brought to their knees in humility, had begged for forgiveness through the atonement of Christ, and had received a remission of their sins. This experience with exercising faith in Christ brought peace of conscience and immense joy. King Benjamin then taught them that the key to continuing to experience that divine joy was to repent, remain humble, and stand "steadfastly in the faith of that which is to come."[87]

---

[82] Doctrine and Covenants 1:32, emphasis added.

[83] For example, see 3 Nephi 9:13-14

[84] See Enos 1:2 (2-8)

[85] Alma 34:17, emphasis added.

[86] Moroni 3:3, emphasis added.

[87] See Mosiah 4:1-3, 10-12; King Benjamin set up a theme early in his sermon of describing the link between faith in the coming of Christ, remission of sin, and immense joy. The Lord God sends prophets to teach the entire world that "whosoever should believe that Christ should come, the same might receive remission of their sins, and rejoice with exceedingly great joy, even as though he had already come among them." (Mosiah 3:13, see also 2 Nephi 25:24-27) These words were written about 150 years before

Understanding the Mysteries of God

By the authority of the Holy Ghost[88], Nephi gave a powerful mini sermon on the process of revelation and related topics. By experience, Nephi knew "he that diligently seeketh shall find; and the mysteries of God shall be unfolded to them, by the power of the Holy Ghost".[89] This is complimentary to the scriptural directive to "ask, and it shall be given unto you; seek, and ye shall find; knock, and it shall be opened unto you."[90]

Nephi's connection between diligent seeking and understanding godly mysteries is also closely related to Ammon's teachings about the importance of penitence in our efforts to comprehend the Divine.[91] In addition to the discussion given previously on this topic, the mysteries of God may also include those parts of your life that seem to interfere with your pursuit of happiness—the job you did not get, the unjust offense you received, the lifelong battle you face, etc. As you follow Nephi's pattern for seeking revelation, you are promised that your understanding will be expanded by the power of the Holy Ghost.

> Christ was on the earth and fulfilling his foreordained ministry in which these people were expressing their faith. We have the benefit of looking back on history to see both their eager anticipation and the fulfillment of the prophesies in the life, ministry, and atoning sacrifice of the Savior. However, we are not dissimilar to those who lived in the B.C. era. Though we read about the life of Christ as history, we also have faith that he will come again. As with the people of King Benjamin, our faith in the anticipation of the next stage of Christ's miraculous work on Earth can be a source of "exceedingly great joy" for all who believe. (See also Alma 16:20 (15-20))

[88] 1 Nephi 10:22

[89] 1 Nephi 10:19 (15-22); These words are written just before the record of Nephi's extended prophetic vision of the Tree of Life, ministry of Christ, and the restoration of Israel, which vision he received by faith. See 1 Nephi 11-14.

[90] Variations of this instruction are in many places throughout the scriptures. This one is quoted from 3 Nephi 14:7.

[91] See Alma 26:21-22

Developing Gifts of the Spirit

The Lord counseled early latter-day saints to "seek ye earnestly the best gifts, always remembering for what they are given"[92] before instructing them about gifts of the Spirit. God gives His children spiritual gifts for the benefit of those who *seek* to keep His commandments. However, the commandment to seek spiritual gifts comes with a word of warning. We must humbly seek after them with real intent, and not with the intent to "consume it upon [our] lusts". In other words, our purpose must be to align our hearts with God's will and not to impose our selfish desires on God's plan.[93]

There are many kinds of spiritual gifts. The scriptures list several important ones, but it is not a complete list. Anytime we see someone (including ourselves) acting with power to help those who are striving to keep the commandments, we can assume that person is exercising a gift of the Spirit. By divine design, everyone has at least one gift, but few have all. This dispersion of gifts obligates us to share what we have been given so that the whole church can have the benefit of all the gifts.[94]

In their earnest quest for spiritual gifts, Paul promised to show the Corinthians "a more excellent way."[95] That way involves each member of the Godhead: we seek after gifts of the Spirit by the Holy Ghost in the name of Christ according to the will of the Father. Successfully petitioning the Godhead in this way requires that we persistently practice gratitude, virtue, and holiness.[96] Moroni taught that spiritual gifts will only go away when our belief goes away. Conversely, when we

---

[92] Doctrine and Covenants 46:8
[93] See Doctrine and Covenants 46:9, 26; see also James 4:3 (3, 6-8)
[94] Doctrine and Covenants 46:11-12; see also 1 Corinthians 12:4, 7, 11-12; Moroni 10:8, 17
[95] 1 Corinthians 12:31
[96] Doctrine and Covenants 46:30-33; see also Doctrine and Covenants 121:45-46

exercise faith, our spiritual gifts will grow. Faith in Christ empowers us to do His will in all things, including experiencing joy.[97]

Happiness is a God-given gift that benefits His children, and anything we know about other spiritual gifts applies to it. Some people seem to be predisposed to experiencing joy, while others have to work harder at it. If you are a naturally joyful person, be grateful for that gift and share it with others in proper ways. If you tend to be more of a melancholy type, recognize your opportunity to exercise faith to develop more meaningful experiences with joy.[98]

---

[97] Moroni 10:19 (19-24); Note that faith cannot exist without its companion virtues, hope, and charity. All three are necessary to experience divine joy and salvation in God's kingdom.

[98] Having one personality type or another is not necessarily good or bad. It is part of God's design for your life. While happiness is a central goal of the Plan of Salvation, God never intended for anyone to experience perpetual happiness in mortality. See "This Vale of Sorrow" for discussion on the necessity of sorrow as well as happiness.

The example of Nephi and Jacob illustrates how happiness may be viewed as a gift of the Spirit. These brothers were separated in age by several years but lived and worked in close proximity for many decades. They experienced many of the same hardships, although from different viewpoints brought about by their age difference. In the twilight of his own life, each man made a statement that suggests a distinct personality and natural tendency for happiness. Nephi concisely observed "we lived after the manner of happiness" (see 2 Nephi 5:27) while Jacob lamented "the time passed away with us...we being a lonesome and a solemn people...wherefore, we did mourn out our days." (See Jacob 7:26) Both men were devoted servants of God and powerful teachers of His gospel. Jacob undoubtedly had as high of standing before God as did his brother. But it seems as though they were working with different tool kits, and that is okay.

Have We Not Reason to Rejoice?

"This is the account of Ammon and his brethren, their journeyings…their sufferings…their sorrows, and their afflictions, and their incomprehensible joy."[99] When we study Ammon's story, his effusive joy and penchant for fainting can be a distraction to the deeper message for all of us seeking greater happiness. Joy was only one facet of his experience, and his profound experiences with joy were possible only because of the equal sorrows he faced.

On their journey, Ammon and his associates suffered depression, "every privation"[100], and "all manner of afflictions." They were cast out, mocked, spit upon, beaten, stoned, and imprisoned. Through all this suffering, they learned to rely on the mercies of God and man for all their physical support. They learned the virtues of diligence, longsuffering, and patience. Most importantly, they learned that God was bigger than any hardship they faced. He delivered them from physical destruction repeatedly. An even greater miracle is that He likewise delivered these young men from spiritual destruction and then enabled them to be the means to bring the same gift to others. They had hoped to bring a few people to salvation, but instead saw thousands accept the Savior and develop incredible love for God and each other. Through all that he had seen, Ammon had a sure witness of the boundless power, wisdom, understanding, comprehension, and mercy of God.[101]

Alma chapter 26 lists at least sixteen distinct reasons that Ammon's heart was "brim with joy", ranging from a generic "great blessings" to the majestic "thousands…brought to sing redeeming love."[102] Ammon's

---

[99] Alma 28:8
[100] Privation is the "absence of what is necessary for comfort"; See "Privation", *American Dictionary of the English Language*. Noah Webster, 14 April 1828.
[101] See Alma 26:26-35
[102] Alma 26:11 (1-15)

joy was neither an accident of circumstance nor an involuntary reward for suffering. When Ammon was made aware of his sinful nature, he chose penitence. When God asked him to do difficult things (and then enabled his success), Ammon chose humility. When terrible suffering presented itself, he chose to seek out happiness.

We are appropriately inspired by a study of the character of Ammon and his companions at the end of their service. They were described as: being brothers in the Lord, having a strong knowledge of truth, being of sound understanding, searchers of the scriptures, those who prayed and fasted much, having the spirit of prophecy and revelation, and being powerful and authoritative teachers.[103] We must remember, though, this is who they *became*. We cannot forget where they started, or their turbulent path to inspiring discipleship and remarkable joy. Mormon recognized their remarkable transformation when he offered the blessing, "may the Lord...bless their souls forever."[104]

This group of missionaries connected with the people they taught in an exceptionally personal way. They had all learned by experience that joy is connected to the gift of eternal life, being born of God, having wicked spirits "rooted out" and receiving the Spirit of God.[105] These people were "wanderers in a strange land", yet God offered irrefutable proof that He was mindful of them. By extension, we can take their story as proof that He is "mindful of every people" and will extend the same grace to *all* "those who will repent and believe on his name."[106]

The details of your own story may look different than Ammon's. You might not be a malicious destroyer of God's kingdom that receives angelic ministration. However, you are certainly in need of redemption and God will call to you by His Spirit. You might not make a foreign king feel indebted to your service, but you can do good in the world. You might not see the conversion of thousands of people, but you are

---

[103] See Alma 17:2-4
[104] Alma 28:8
[105] See Alma 22:15 and Alma 26:17-20
[106] Alma 26:35-37

someone who God can use in bringing about the salvation of others. When you follow Ammon's example of penitence, humility and diligence, you too will see the goodness of the Lord to answer your prayers.[107] You too will witness God's integrity to "[verify] his word unto [you] in every particular".[108] You too will be so filled with praise for God that words will feel inadequate.[109] And somewhere along the way, you too may just find happiness.

Have you not reason to rejoice?[110]

---

[107] See Alma 17:9-11
[108] Alma 25:17
[109] See Alma 26:16
[110] See Alma 26:35

LIVING AFTER THE MANNER OF HAPPINESS

Most of what we know about Nephi's life history comes from his early years. When his family made their exodus from Jerusalem in 600 B.C., we know he was "exceedingly young"[1] but still old enough to have been trusted to retrieve the brass plates from Laban, mistaken for Laban, seen as a leader and spiritually mature enough to receive the vision of the tree of life and other revelations. It is safe to assume he was in his late teens or early twenties when their journey started. It took about eleven years to travel to the Promised Land[2] but from there, his record focuses more on spiritual matters (e.g., quoting Isaiah) and less on recording history, as commanded by God.[3] Thirty years after leaving Jerusalem (when he would have been about fifty years old) he gave a brief history of his people's first two decades in the Promised Land.[4] Near the end of this part of the record, he made a summary observation that, "we lived after the manner of happiness."[5]

Nephi's record gives several hints into what living "after the manner of happiness" may have meant for him. For example, we know that his people were commandment keepers. They grew their own food, were prepared to protect themselves from an attack, and were industrious. They had a temple as a prominent feature of their community and had priesthood leaders and gospel teachers. This was a period of prosperity

---

[1] 1 Nephi 2:16
[2] See year estimation given in 1 Nephi 18:23 of the standard edition of the Book of Mormon
[3] See 2 Nephi 5:29-33
[4] See 2 Nephi 5:28 (5-28)
[5] 2 Nephi 5:27

for them, but it came after extensive difficulties with their journey to the Promised Land and continued conflicts with the Lamanites.[6]

The Book of Mormon tells the story of another society centuries later that also experienced a notable degree of happiness because of the way they lived. It was said of them, "there could not be a happier people among all the people who had been created by the hand of God."[7] For this society, living "after the manner of happiness" meant abolishing all contention, envying, strife, and sin. They were repentant, lived covenant lives, and worshipped together. They exercised faith and witnessed miracles. They had no social divisions, were united as children of Christ, and had the love of God dwelling in their hearts. The Lord blessed them "in all their doings" and they prospered in this condition for 75 years.[8]

For three years after the destruction of the people of Ammoniah, the Nephites experienced a period of peace and notable establishment of the Church of God. During this time, Alma, Amulek and other missionaries traveled broadly among the Nephites and freely taught repentance and encouraged faith in the coming of the Son of God. Because there was no discrimination in choosing whom they taught pure doctrine, the establishment of the Church was widespread among all Nephites. Furthermore, the lack of prejudice fostered a sense of equality that allowed the Spirit of the Lord to be poured out on them.[9] This Spirit came to prepare them to be taught the gospel that Christ would preach

---

[6] See 2 Nephi 5:4-26

[7] 4 Nephi 1:16

[8] See 4 Nephi 1:15-18 (1-18); This era of happiness was the first generation of those who witnessed Christ's ministry in the Americas. Though their children and grandchildren were raised in an idyllic setting, the afterglow of Christ's ministry faded with those who were firsthand witnesses, and wickedness more easily crept back into the civilization.

[9] A consequence of the pouring out of the Lord's Spirit was a "victory over the devil." The devil only has as much power as the children of God give him by use of their agency.

when He ministered among them.[10] The anticipation of Christ's ministry in the Americas, coupled with a knowledge that they were grafted into the house of Israel, was a source of "great joy and gladness" for the people.[11]

There is clearly a pattern where righteousness is a predecessor to happiness. In spelling out the causes that motivated the Nephites to defend themselves in battle, Captain Moroni argued that they owed *all* their happiness to the "maintenance of the sacred word of God."[12] Lehi taught that happiness can only exist as the fruit of righteousness.[13] Proverbs proclaims, "righteousness exalteth a nation"[14] and the Lord declared through Joseph Smith that "he who doeth righteousness shall receive...peace in this world, and eternal life in the world to come."[15] Alma taught his son Corianton that "wickedness never was happiness" and anything that is contrary to God's nature is contrary to the nature of happiness[16]. By implication, God's nature is the very nature of happiness.

In short, if you want to find happiness, you need to find God.

Such a statement does not seem to square well with our mortal experience. We all know people who have found great happiness in life off—maybe after leaving—the covenant path. Certainly, there are

---

[10] Bear in mind that this was about 112 years prior to Christ's ministry in Bountiful; see 3 Nephi 11-26

[11] See Alma 16:12-21; Alma was leading this transformation among the Nephites in the final years of the miraculous work the sons of Mosiah facilitated among the Lamanites, which culminated with them leading a group of Lamanite refugees to be assimilated into Nephite society. Perhaps the culture of equality, fostered by a love of God, the Nephites developed during these years was a necessary preparation for receiving the Anti-Nephi-Lehis without prejudice. See Alma 27:21-27.

[12] Alma 44:5

[13] See 2 Nephi 2:13 (10-13)

[14] Proverbs 14:34

[15] Doctrine and Covenants 59:23

[16] Alma 41:10-11; See also Helaman 13:38

practical implications of being wholly committed to living a holy life that seem to interfere with one's pursuit of happiness. How would your social connections be different if you accepted the world's standards on chastity or the Word of Wisdom? What would you do with the extra money in your budget that did not go towards tithing and other offerings? How else could you spend the time you devote to worship and service in the church on Sunday and throughout the week? The answers to all these questions point in the same direction: living the gospel can take away from the happiness the world has to offer.

In his assessment of the state of the Nephites in their final (and unsuccessful) fight for survival, Mormon implies that the Lord will sometimes *allow* happiness in sin.[17] Certainly, people in the great and spacious building were laughing, enjoying the company, and otherwise having a fun time. There is a particular degree of freedom in adopting the guiltless philosophy, "eat, drink, and be merry...for tomorrow we die."[18] But there is a catch. There is *always* a catch.

HAPPINESS AND MORTALITY

When the Savior ministered among the Nephites, he taught several important lessons related to establishing His church. One of those lessons was the importance of being built on His gospel. The alternative is to have a church built on the works of men, or the devil. In the latter case, "they may have joy in their works *for a season*, and by and by the end cometh, and they are hewn down and cast into the fire, from whence there is no return."[19] This teaching establishes an important principle that no work can survive beyond the power or authority by which it was created.

Our mortal condition is, by nature of the fall of Adam and Eve, bound by the effects of time. As with a church, happiness from mortal

---

[17] See Mormon 2:13 (12-14)
[18] 2 Nephi 28:8
[19] 3 Nephi 27:11 (9-12), emphasis added.

things cannot outlast mortality. Buildings will crumble. Paintings will fade. Sports cars will rust. Even the most elegant banquets will leave you hungry in the morning. This principle extends to less-tangible creations, too. Investment funds are meaningless to the owner at death. Social media followers will be drawn to someone new. Roars of applause will fade into time and space. Mighty businesses will eventually fall into oblivion. Most marriages are guaranteed only "until death do you part."

The happiness we receive from any of these examples can be real, valid, and not necessarily "bad." But the reward of any worldly pursuit is self-contained.[20] A sincere seeker of happiness must understand the temporary shelf life of this kind of joy.[21]

Eternal joy can only come from the pattern given by "the high and lofty One that inhabiteth eternity... [who dwells with those] of a contrite and humble spirit." In that holy place, God promises to "revive the spirit of the humble, and to revive the heart of the contrite ones." His promise extends to blessings of healing, restoration of comforts, and peace.[22] In other words, living with God means eternal happiness.

As we talk about eternal joy being possible only when it comes from an eternal source, lasting joy may feel distant and unattainable—something reserved only for the eternities when we will dwell with God in paradise. It is critical to remember, though, that *right now* is part of eternity. You can choose to live with God *right now*. Because of that, God's eternal offerings of peace, restoration, healing, comfort, and happiness are available to you in this moment.

We "are free to choose liberty and eternal life, through the great Mediator of all men, or to choose captivity and death, according to the captivity and power of the devil"[23]. That choice is best made in mortality

---

[20] See 3 Nephi 13: 2, 5, 16
[21] See Mormon 8:38
[22] Isaiah 57:15 (15-21)
[23] 2 Nephi 2:27

"which is given us to *prepare for eternity*" and before "the night of darkness wherein there can be no labor performed."[24]

Happiness in mortality is not a frail coverup of all the pains associated with our fallen condition—it is a central purpose of our life on earth. President Russell M. Nelson described the apparent paradox of joy being a central purpose of our fallen world in this way:

> *Clearly, Lehi knew opposition, anxiety, heartache, pain, disappointment, and sorrow. Yet he declared boldly and without reservation a principle as revealed by the Lord: "Men are, that they might have joy." Imagine! Of all the words he could have used to describe the nature and purpose of our lives here in mortality, he chose the word joy!*
>
> *...Just as the Savior offers peace that "passeth all understanding," He also offers an intensity, depth, and breadth of joy that defy human logic or mortal comprehension. For example, it doesn't seem possible to feel joy when your child suffers with an incurable illness or when you lose your job or when your spouse betrays you. Yet that is precisely the joy the Savior offers. His joy is constant, assuring us that our "afflictions shall be but a small moment" and be consecrated to our gain."*[25]

A common refrain shouted from the terraces of the great and spacious building is "come with us and you will be free." The world will have you focus on the experiences you miss in following the Savior, pointing to discipleship as a type of bondage that prevents you from

---

[24] Alma 34:33, emphasis added.
[25] Russell M. Nelson, "Joy and Spiritual Survival", *Liahona*, November 2016, 81-84.

experiencing true joy.[26] This philosophy is a maliciously crafted deception because it perverts the truth. It takes the realities of the consequences of sin and projects them on to faithful discipleship. It is a classic play of the Adversary, who "call[s] evil good, and good evil."[27]

Returning to the examples given earlier, those who accept and live the Lord's standards on chastity will discover the truth of this statement:

> *Our Heavenly Father has given us the law of chastity for our protection. Obedience to this law is essential to personal peace and strength of character and to happiness in the home. Those who keep themselves sexually pure will avoid the spiritual and emotional damage that always comes from sharing physical intimacies with someone outside of marriage. Those who keep themselves sexually pure will be sensitive to the Holy Ghost's guidance, strength, comfort, and protection and will fulfill an important requirement for receiving a temple recommend and participating in temple ordinances.*[28]

Furthermore, they will "progress toward perfection and ultimately realize their divine destiny as heirs of eternal life"[29], even though they may be set at odds with popular social opinions.

Those who valiantly obey the Word of Wisdom "shall receive health in their navel and marrow to their bones; And shall find wisdom and great treasures of knowledge, even hidden treasures; And shall run and not be weary, and shall walk and not faint." They are further promised, "the destroying angel shall pass by them...and not slay them."[30]

---

[26] See 3 Nephi 24:14-15
[27] Isaiah 5:20
[28] See "Chastity" in Gospel Topics, ChurchofJesusChrist.org
[29] "The Family: A Proclamation to the World," ChurchofJesusChrist.org
[30] Doctrine and Covenants 89:18-21

However, adhering to the Word of Wisdom could potentially put them in awkward social situations when they do not conform to cultural norms.

To those who faithfully live the law of tithing, the Lord of Hosts promises to:

> Open you the windows of heaven, and pour you out a blessing, that there shall not be room enough to receive it. And I will rebuke the devourer for your sakes, and he shall not destroy the fruits of your ground; neither shall your vine cast her fruit before the time in the field, saith the Lord of hosts. And all nations shall call you blessed: for ye shall be a delightsome land.[31]

However, sacrificing a part of one's income to the Lord may initially stretch budgets and cause one to go without luxuries, or even necessities for a time in extreme cases.

When we gather in worship and service in the Lord's church, "a book of remembrance [is] written before [the Lord] for them that feared the Lord, and that thought upon his name. And they shall be mine, saith the Lord of Hosts, in that day when I make up my jewels; and I will spare them as a man spareth his own son that serveth him. Then shall ye return and discern between the righteous and the wicked, between him that serveth God and him that serveth him not."[32] Furthermore, fellow worshipers often find "their hearts knit together in unity and in love one towards another."[33] However, whole-hearted service and worship take significant commitments of time that could be spent on other pursuits of recreation or self-development.

---

[31] Malachi 3:10-12
[32] 3 Nephi 24:16-18
[33] Mosiah 18:21

In short, living the gospel can take away from the happiness the world has to offer. But it will always yield something more eternally grand.[34]

> *Wherefore, do not spend money for that which is of no worth, nor your labor for that which cannot satisfy. Hearken diligently unto me, and remember the words which I have spoken; and come unto the Holy One of Israel, and feast upon that which perisheth not, neither can be corrupted, and let your soul delight in fatness.*[35]
>
> *Lay not up for yourselves treasures upon earth, where moth and rust doth corrupt, and where thieves break through and steal: But lay up for yourselves treasures in heaven, where neither moth nor rust doth corrupt, and where thieves do not break through nor steal.*[36]

King Benjamin invited his people to, "consider on the blessed and happy state of those that keep the commandments of God. For behold, they are blessed in all things, both temporal and spiritual." These blessings Benjamin promised for righteous living apply to mortality. The King also reminded them—and us—that if commandment keepers "hold out faithful to the end they are received into heaven, that thereby they may dwell with God in a state of never-ending happiness."[37]

Christ pleads with anyone who will listen, "Come unto me, all ye that labour and are heavy laden" then promises, "I will give you rest. Take my yoke upon you, and learn of me; for I am meek and lowly in heart: and ye shall find rest unto your souls."[38]

---

[34] See Genesis 25:29-34
[35] 2 Nephi 9:51
[36] Matthew 6:19-20 (19-33)
[37] Mosiah 2:41
[38] Matthew 11:28-29

It is inherent in our divine DNA to yearn for happiness. In this perpetual and universal pursuit, humanity has found many means (divinely inspired and otherwise) to experience various degrees of joy. Works of mortal hands can only produce happiness that is limited to mortality. We can look to the scriptures for godly patterns others have discovered to find happiness that is valid now and willast into eternity. However, even divinely given principles can be obstacles if they are applied incorrectly or inconsistently.[39]

The only sure way to find genuine, lasting joy is in the persistent, careful, and humble application of the eternal principles of our Heavenly Father's Plan of Salvation. To "live after the manner of happiness"—true, eternal happiness—is to live after the manner of Christ.

---

[39] See Helaman 12:1-2 (1-7, 20-26) for one example of divinely given prosperity becoming an obstacle.

THIS VALE OF SORROW

A comprehensive study of happiness and joy is incomplete without careful consideration of their opposites, namely sorrow and mourning. As exemplified by the account of Adam and Eve eating the forbidden fruit, we can perceive joy only when contrasted against misery.[1] If eternal laws demand there "must be an opposition in all things"[2], and "men are, that they might have joy"[3] then sorrow and mourning are requisite elements of our mortal experience. The humble seeker of happiness will recognize the critical role of unpleasant experiences and emotions as evidence of the "wisdom of him who knoweth all things"[4] who is the "author of eternal salvation."[5]

Our natural tendency is to view "bad things" as inherently being of no worth. Our response to this assumption can take many different forms. On one end of the spectrum, we may shun negative experiences and perpetually seek green grass and blue skies. Conversely, there are those who have come to accept sorrows as an inevitable part of life, but with the understanding that they must be evidence of their own poor choices or an unjust God. While each approach has shadows of truth, neither is healthy nor doctrinally supported. The first leads to a life of naïveté, while the latter fosters self-pity. Both stifle the growth we need to experience in life.

---

[1] See 2 Nephi 2:23 and Moses 5:10-11
[2] 2 Nephi 2:11 (10-13)
[3] 2 Nephi 2:25
[4] 2 Nephi 2:24
[5] Hebrews 5:9

Mourning in mortality is universal. Alma metaphorically described our life on earth as "this vale [or valley] of sorrow."[6] In similar language, the Psalmist described walking "through the valley of the shadow of death"[7] as part of the mortal experience. A simple listing of the sorrows individuals have experienced would fill countless volumes. Furthermore, any mortal could fill many books with a detailed accounting of their personal sorrows, but only those sorrows within the power of expression of written language.

With sorrow being such a pervasive part of the human experience, accepting the assumption that it is bad carries a conclusion that, if God does indeed exist, He is either cruel or incapable of influence in the world He created. The alternative view is that sorrow is an intentional and beneficial (if incomprehensible) element of our mortal experience. With a faith-filled perspective, we understand that a meaningful mortal experience cannot be devoid of sorrow.

The Book of Mormon is filled with stories of individuals and societies who grappled with sorrow, mourning, and misery. A study of their experiences and teachings reveals a heavenly framework to understand our own encounters with trials and tribulations.

Death and Wickedness

The Book of Mormon has two primary themes as sources of sorrow. The first is war and the second is wickedness. These themes reflect the two major effects of the fall of Adam and Eve, namely physical and spiritual death. Our modern-day sorrows are often related to these same themes. The sorrows we face from various degrees of illness, tragedy, and violence—or the anticipation of them—are all connected to our fear of physical death and the fragility of life. When our sorrow is related to the virtue of ourselves or others, it reflects our faith in God's eternal promises and the possibility that we may not experience all that the

---

[6] Alma 37:45
[7] Psalm 23:4

Father has in store for us. Studying the sorrows related to physical and spiritual death in the Book of Mormon can help us to contextualize our own grief.

The people of Limhi are just one of many groups in the Book of Mormon who were well acquainted with the sorrows of mortality, including war. This Nephite sub-society formed when a group of Nephites left Zarahemla to re-inhabit lands where Lehi's family first landed on the continent. Unfortunately, these lands were Lamanite territory, and it was not as easy as pitching a tent and claiming it as their own. Before they had even made it to their target destination, they were plagued by internal strife that resulted in many deaths.

Eventually, the Lamanites agreed to give part of their land to these Nephites, but not for free. The Lamanites levied heavy taxes on them, kept them under guard and would sometimes wage unprovoked battles. They lived in these circumstances for about 80 years and two more generations. In this time, they had at least seven skirmishes with the Lamanites. Additionally, the middle generation (led by King Noah) was very wicked. Because of Noah's wickedness, they suffered internal violence and their society splintered into three separate groups. Two of those groups (one led by Limhi and the other by Alma) were finally able to escape their captors and find peace once again in Zarahemla.

Near the end of their captivity, Limhi lamented "Great are the reasons which we have to mourn; for behold how many of our brethren have been slain, and their blood has been spilt in vain, and all because of iniquity."[8] If the bondage and death they had suffered was not sorrowful enough, their feelings of grief were compounded by the sentiment that it was all a result of pride and sin.[9]

---

[8] Mosiah 7:24 (21-26)

[9] See Mosiah 7-22, especially chapters 9 and 21; Consider the especially fragile state Limhi would have been in as the leader who was tasked with leading the people out of bondage, but with the heritage of being the grandson of Zeniff and son of Noah.

There are many examples of people mourning over the spiritual death of others. In the years leading up to Christ's coming, there was rampant apostasy, which caused great sorrow for the faithful people. This sorrow was especially poignant for the older generations of Lamanites who saw the rising generation flattered away into the hollow promises of the Gadianton robbers.[10]

Similarly, Christ himself expressed sorrow for apostasy. He foresaw a future generation who would sell Him for money and the corruptible things of the world, and thus be "led away captive" by Satan.[11]

Mormon was surrounded by gross wickedness and violence. Yet, he knew it was his duty to preserve an honest record of his people. Nevertheless, he was judicious in what he recorded to shield us, his target audience, from sorrow too great to bear.[12]

Complex Feelings

Emotional reactions reflect our environment. Our lived experience, relationships with others, and current energy level all affect our response to anything that happens. Imagine your response to someone stepping on your toe. How does your response change if it happens in the temple versus a crowded shopping mall? What if it is a dance partner versus an obnoxious kid on the playground? Maybe it is someone walking next to you and stumbles to the ground, and they squish your toe but bump their head. Maybe the same guy walks by your cubicle at work and steps on your same toe every day, and you have come to accept it as part of your daily routine.

In any of these cases, your toe would hurt the same amount. Your kneejerk reaction may even be similar each time; but as your understanding of the situation settles in, your emotional reaction and

---

[10] See Helaman 6:33 (26-33) and 3 Nephi 1:29 (27-30)
[11] 3 Nephi 27:32 (30-32)
[12] See Mormon 5:8-9

subsequent use of agency will likely vary. We cannot expect our emotional reactions to be predictable without being certain we understand all relevant circumstances. Predicting (or dictating) emotions is difficult enough when doing so for ourselves but becomes much more problematic when doing so for someone else.

Picture in your mind a well-blended color wheel fading from red to orange, yellow, green, blue, purple, and back to red. Besides an outer ring with these bright colors, the inner part of the circle blends colors across from each other to create a swirl of muted versions of the outer colors. There is an infinite number of colors in this wheel. Now picture each of those colors fading gradually to white in one direction and to black in the other direction. Infinite just got bigger, and it all started with just eight named colors. It becomes impossible to label these colors without describing mixes of the base colors, adding "-ish," or using vocabulary that is unfamiliar to most people.

Interpreting color can be incredibly complicated. The way we perceive colors can change based on the other colors around them. Two people looking at the same color palette may insist on different names for the colors they see, based on their own perspective and bias. For most of us, this complexity of color can be overwhelming to the point of concluding it is all inconsequential. However, visual artists are experts in the spectrum of color. Rather than being overwhelmed by its complexity, they use the subtilties of color to create beautiful things for the rest of us to enjoy.

Like the color wheel you just visualized, human emotion is multi-dimensional and often experienced on a spectrum. It is seldom possible to cleanly sort all our feelings into "happy" and "sad" buckets. We may recognize elements of named emotions, but there are many intermediate feelings that are not always easy to label. Mixed with the element of time and the complexities of circumstance discussed previously, it is easy to see how complicated emotions can be. Like painters or photographers, people who invest the effort to learn the value of the full emotional spectrum will be able to see and create beauty out of complex situations.

As you may expect, the Book of Mormon has several beautiful examples of people who wrestled with complicated feelings, and there is much we can learn from their experiences. Picture yourself in the shoes of each of these scriptural heroes and imagine how you would respond to their circumstances.

Nephi was shown a grand vision of the condescension of the Lord and rejoiced in God's greatness. In the same moment, his heart wept, and his soul grieved because of his iniquities and weakness.[13]

Moroni experienced a similar complexity of emotion when he was simultaneously filled with courage, joy, mourning (and perhaps a little embarrassment) when he received Pahoran's letter confirming his faithfulness, extending his forgiveness, and expressing alarm over a coup.[14]

King Mosiah welcomed two groups of refugees (led by Alma and Limhi) into his society in Zarahemla. Both groups originated from the people of Zeniff, who had separated from Zarahemla two generations previously. When these people were welcomed back "home," Mosiah read their records publicly. The people responded with wonder, amazement, joy, sorrow, gratitude, praise, pain, and anguish—all at once.[15] Something similar happened when King Mosiah translated the Jaredite records and learned of their demise. In this case, we know he mourned for their destruction at the same time he rejoiced in his newfound knowledge.[16]

The missionary experiences of Alma, Ammon, and their associates illustrate how joy often only comes after a period of sorrow, and both emotions can be centered around experiences with the same people. Alma expressed this sentiment related to the people in his hometown of Zarahemla.[17] After being alarmed at their pride and wickedness, Alma

---

[13] See 2 Nephi 4:17,26 (16-35)
[14] See Alma 62:1-2 (see also Alma 59-61)
[15] See Mosiah 25:7-12
[16] See Mosiah 28:18 (17-18)
[17] See Alma 7:5

relinquished his responsibilities in government so that he could devote himself entirely to the ministry. After diligent effort, he saw the people repent and return to discipleship.[18]

Ammon saw this contrast of feelings in a notable way in relation to the Lamanites. He had grown up in a culture that pointed to the Lamanites as the overarching source of mourning. They were wicked, rebellious, and aggressive towards Ammon's people. When Ammon saw the Spirit of the Lord moving among them, convincing them of the same Redeemer that Ammon knew and loved, his subsequent joy was overwhelming.[19]

Sometimes, complex feelings are not associated with innately "bad" experiences but are internal wrestles as our immortal spirits grasp for understanding in this mortal world. When Christ privately ministered to His twelve chosen disciples in Bountiful, three of them "sorrowed" because they were hesitant to share their desires with the Savior. While the rest of the group openly expressed their wishes to return to heaven as soon as they could, the minority group had equally righteous, but more unorthodox desires. They wanted to remain on earth until Christ comes again so that they could continue ministering among the children of God. As the desires of their hearts fought against fears of what others might have thought, Christ reminded them that He already knew what they were thinking and then granted their wishes. Not only were they validated in their unorthodoxy but were blessed more so because of it.[20]

ANTIDOTES FOR SORROW

With all the discussion about sorrow in the Book of Mormon, the text does not leave us helpless. There are several practical examples of people who grappled with sorrow and showed us tools we can all apply to counteract its effects.

---

[18] See Alma 4:6-20, Alma 5-6
[19] See Alma 19:14 and 28:8
[20] See 3 Nephi 28:5 (1-12)

As part of his record keeping, Jacob clearly outlined his purposes in completing the challenging task of preserving the sacred records. He wanted future generations to remember earlier generations with joy and not "sorrow, neither with contempt." The way to do that was with education. By taking charge of the records, Jacob could ensure his experiences and faith would be documented in a lasting first-person account, and not subject to the volatility and corruptibility of memory alone.[21] The people of Mosiah also discovered the connection between knowledge and joy when they learned about the Jaredites.[22]

In his final words to his rebellious sons, Lehi pleaded for them to be on their best behavior so that he could die with joy and not sorrow. He invited them to, "[Awake and] arise from the dust...and be men." By extension, his invitation included pleas to "remember to observe the statutes and judgements of the Lord," "be determined in one mind and in one heart, united in all things", and to "put on the armor of righteousness". In other words, Lehi told his sons to shake off the filth of the world and embrace righteousness. Lehi begged these things for the sake of his own happiness, but happiness surely would have also come to Laman and Lemuel had they heeded the counsel.[23]

Alma experienced many sorrows in his ministry work, often because of the apostasy of his people and rejection of his teachings. Nevertheless, he demonstrated at least three strategies to deal with sorrow. These tools are related and elements of each can be found in the following: The first was to recognize the constant support of the Spirit even when he was "very sorrowful".[24] The second was to pray earnestly for comfort, strength, and patience.[25] The third tool was to act within the powers of his own control. For example, when he felt that his

---

[21] Jacob 4:3 (1-4)
[22] See Mosiah 28:18 (11-18); see also Omni 1:20, Mosiah 8:8-14, Ether 1:1-5
[23] 2 Nephi 1:21 (16-23)
[24] See Alma 4:15 (15-16, 19)
[25] See Alma 31:24, 30-37

teachings to the people were fruitless, he focused on teaching his sons and empowering them to fulfill their own duties in life.[26]

One of his sons was Helaman, who later became an important military commander. Even as Helaman faced many difficulties in this service, he found positive things to be happy about. He was not naïve about his challenges and did not shy away from sharing them with others, but he was also deliberate in celebrating the things for which he could be grateful.[27]

Righteousness and Sorrow

First through the Old Testament prophet Malachi, and then to the people in Bountiful, the Lord observed that rebellious people will sometimes lament, "It is vain to serve God: and what profit is it that we have kept his ordinance, and that we have walked mournfully before the Lord of hosts? And now we call the proud happy; yea, they that work wickedness are set up; yea, they that tempt God are even delivered."[28]

This argument is halfway valid. Devoted discipleship can look and feel like mournful walking at times. Conversely, wicked people sometimes have fortunate things happen to them. Our Father in Heaven "sendeth rain on the just and on the unjust."[29] Sometimes rain is a welcomed gift from heaven as it revitalizes the ground and enables new life. Sometimes rain is devastating as floods wipe away crops and homes. Regardless of the status of your discipleship, you will experience the same positive or negative results from natural phenomena like rain. Neither happiness and sorrow, nor fortune and tragedy are indicative of your standing before God. They are indicative of being human.

---

[26] See Alma 35:15-16 (see also Alma 36-42)
[27] See Alma 56:9-11, 17
[28] Malachi 3:14-15; see also 3 Nephi 24:14-15
[29] Matthew 5:45

Righteousness has never been a guaranteed means to avoid all the sorrows of life. As will be discussed later, sorrow is a requisite element of discipleship. Many of our great scriptural heroes were subjected to trials small and great. We revere them because of their continued faithfulness through—not around—hardship. Consider these examples from the Book of Mormon:

The story of Lehi leading his family out of Jerusalem is one of the most vivid accounts in the Book of Mormon illustrating how righteous people are not immune to sorrows. Lehi was a prophet and had seen God on His throne. It was because of his testimony of the coming Messiah that his life was threatened and he had to take his family elsewhere.[30] The sons of Lehi and Sariah followed the commandments of God in going back to Jerusalem to retrieve the brass plates, but doing so caused great grief for their mother.[31] Though the family was assured of the Lord's guiding hand in their journey,[32] their physical afflictions pushed even Lehi to a breaking point and he was subsequently chastened by the Lord.[33] The death of Ishmael was a tremendous source of sorrow for his daughters.[34] The hardened hearts of Laman and Lemuel were a persistent source of fear, sorrow, and anxiety for Nephi,[35] Lehi,[36] Jacob[37] and most everyone else in the company. Nevertheless, these two oldest sons were known to sorrow unto repentance on occasion.[38] Nephi was plagued by failure[39] and abuse[40] as

---

[30] See 1 Nephi 1:8, 18-20

[31] See 1 Nephi 3:2-4; 5:1-3

[32] See 1 Nephi 17:13-14

[33] See 1 Nephi 16:20-25

[34] See 1 Nephi 16:34-36

[35] See 1 Nephi 17:19, see also 2 Nephi 1:24

[36] See 2 Nephi 1:17, 21

[37] See 2 Nephi 2:1

[38] See 1 Nephi 7:20

[39] For example, see 1 Nephi 3:14

[40] For example, see 1 Nephi 18:11

he strived to keep the commandments of the Lord. Joseph knew nothing but sorrow and affliction from the time he was born.[41]

Near the end of his life, Nephi mourned for the "unbelief, and the wickedness, and the ignorance, and the stiffneckedness of men".[42] Similarly, Jacob punctuated their entire history with a description of being, "a lonesome and a solemn people, cast out...born in tribulation...and hated...wherefore, we did mourn out our days".[43] Despite all this, there is little doubt of the righteousness of Lehi, Nephi, or Jacob, nor of the sacred value of their writings.

As poignant as the story of Lehi's family may be, there are many other less prevalent examples of righteous people who suffered various degrees of sorrow.

Abish and her father had been converted to the Lord for many years. But as a servant to the Lamanite queen, she had to keep her faith internalized because the people around her would have been unsympathetic to her convictions. When King Lamoni, the queen, and their servants began to have their own remarkable conversions, Abish's excitement was uncontainable. She ran through the streets inviting people to come to see the miraculous events. However, her elation collapsed into despair when the scene became one of contention instead of conversion for the townspeople. With tears running down her cheeks, her faith prevailed as she raised her queen up from the ground so that she could testify to the people.[44]

There was a small contingent of people who steadfastly believed in the prophecies of Samuel and other prophets concerning the signs of Christ's birth. When the predicted time was close but not passed, the skeptics first mocked and then threatened the believers with death.

---

[41] See 2 Nephi 3:1
[42] 2 Nephi 32:7
[43] Jacob 7:26
[44] See Alma 19:16-18, 28-29

Surely, they had cause to sorrow, especially before Nephi prayed and received confirmation that the sign was about to be given.[45]

The Jaredite king Omer was born into royalty and a culture of righteousness. However, he had a son named Jared (not the namesake of the civilization) who was driven by brazen greed and pride. Jared twice forced control of the kingdom from his father, once by a military coup and another time more subtly by the introduction of a secretive order into Jaredite society. Both rebellions were eventually reversed, and a righteous son Emer was placed on the throne in Omer's stead. When Omer died, it was noted he had "seen exceedingly many days, which were full of sorrow."[46]

Coriantumr was another Jaredite king who had been warned of his wickedness by the prophet Ether. He not only rejected Ether but tried to kill him. Eventually, Coriantumr remembered the words of warning and repented. Unfortunately, that day of awakening did not come until two million of his people were killed in a battle he had led. By that point, conditions were so bad that "his soul mourned and refused to be comforted," despite his desires to repent. Furthermore, the war was endemic, and he eventually saw the death of every person on both sides of the conflict until he was the sole survivor.[47] This once mighty king became a lonesome vagabond and lived with the people in Zarahemla for a brief time.[48]

Mormon holds a seat of honor in the Righteous Sorrowers Hall of Fame. At age 10, Mormon was recognized as a "sober child, and…quick to observe" and was given stewardship for all Nephite records.[49] Five years later, at 15, he was "visited of the Lord, and tasted and knew of the goodness of Jesus" despite the pervasively wicked culture by which he was surrounded. Though he wanted to preach repentance, he was

---

[45] See 3 Nephi 1:7, 10 (4-13)
[46] Ether 9:15; See also Ether 7:27, 8:1-18, 9:1-15
[47] See Ether 15:1-3; See also Ether 12:1-5; 13:2, 15-31; 14:1-31; 15:1-32
[48] See Omni 1:21
[49] See Mormon 1:2-4

forbidden from doing so because the hearts of the people were so hardened.[50] In this same year, he was appointed chief leader of the Nephite armies and led them into battle.[51] The next 59 years of Mormon's life were filled with pleas to repent that proved to be fruitless and leading battles that decimated his people. He had also been faithful in his duty to abridge, protect, and add to the sacred records with a hope that future people (i.e., *you*) could learn from them.[52] At 74 years old, his "soul was rent with anguish" and cried out:

> *O ye fair ones, how could ye have departed from the ways of the Lord! O ye fair ones, how could ye have rejected that Jesus, who stood with open arms to receive you! Behold, if ye had not done this, ye would not have fallen. But behold, ye are fallen, and I mourn your loss. O ye fair sons and daughters, ye fathers and mothers, ye husbands and wives, ye fair ones, how is it that ye could have fallen! But behold, ye are gone, and my sorrows cannot bring your return.*[53]

Evolution of Sorrow

Tragedy and its associated mourning put us in a place of vulnerability. When comforts are stripped away, our inner selves are exposed in unique ways. Such openness can become a transitory step either to fear or rejoicing, depending on how one's faith is exercised while mourning. Sorrow may be unavoidable, but misery is optional.

The Book of Mormon has several negative and positive examples of the evolution of sorrow. In some cases, tragedy led individuals into

---

[50] Mormon 1:15 (13-19); Mormon had tasted the fruit of the tree of life. The account of Lehi's vision would have felt relatable as he abridged the record. See 1 Nephi 8:11-12, 11:8, 21-23, 15:36.
[51] See Mormon 2:1-2
[52] See Mormon 2-6 and Words of Mormon 1:1-8
[53] Mormon 6:17-20 (16-22)

misery and sin. Conversely, we also read about those who experienced similar (even the same) tragedies but were led into greater faith and eventual joy.[54]

NEGATIVE EXAMPLES

When Ishmael died enroute to the Promised Land, his daughters rightly mourned his loss. That event seems to have been an impetus for them to recall every affliction they had suffered since leaving their home in Jerusalem. They complained against Lehi and Nephi, laying blame for their circumstances on them. The negativity of Ishmael's daughters spread to their husbands and brothers, who started conspiring to kill Lehi and Nephi. What started as mourning lead to murmuring and then to threats of violence.[55]

As discussed previously, the early Jaredite king Jared was never an example of righteousness. By flattery, he won over half the kingdom from his father Omer, and then captured him as a prisoner of war. Jared's siblings saw the injustice of that and led a successful counteroffensive to win back their father's kingdom. Out of sheer mercy, they spared the life of their brother, even though it was in their hands. Nevertheless, Jared's sorrow for losing control of the kingdom he had briefly held would not subside. His desires for the glories of the world were greater than his sense of right and wrong, or gratitude for his merciful siblings. In his prideful sorrow, he devised a plan to resurrect ancient secret orders, and by them assassinate his father and then return to power.[56]

The noble Captain Moroni had already been through many difficulties in a long war when a surprise attack by the Lamanites resulted in an "exceedingly great slaughter" and then the complete loss of the city of Nephihah. This loss was especially demoralizing because Moroni had supposed that the government would have sent more

---

[54] For example, see Alma 28:11-12
[55] See 1 Nephi 16:34-38
[56] See Ether 8:7-10 (1-19)

warriors to defend that city, and it should have been an easy defense. From his disappointment, sorrow, then doubt, and then anger grew.[57] In his anger, Moroni, wrote a scathing letter to the chief judge Pahoran, making accusations that later proved to be unfounded. Fortunately, Moroni repented.[58]

Near the demise of Nephite civilization, they and the Lamanites were locked in prolonged and difficult battle. The Nephites mourned greatly and began to repent, but the brutality of war and pervasive sinful culture were too much to bear. Their sorrow was primarily tied to the Lord's refusal to always let them take happiness in sin. Instead of turning their hearts to the mercies of the Lord, they cursed God and clung to their swords in the ultimate battle for their lives and civilization. Mormon watched helplessly as the bodies of his people—associates, friends, and family—were "heaped up as dung" as they lost their fight in "open rebellion against their God." While Mormon experienced the same things as his people (compounded by his sorrow for their rebellion) his faith was such to still know he would be "lifted up at the last day."[59]

Positive Examples

The example of Mormon staying faithful during the same circumstances that caused others to spiral into rebellion is just one such instance in the Book of Mormon. As dismal as the former examples may be, the sacred record also has many examples of people who let tragedy lead them into positive action.

The people of Limhi were subjects to the Lamanites, being taxed of half of their possessions and under constant guard.[60] Two years later[61], the Lamanites launched an unjust battle on Limhi's people. Eventually,

---

[57] See Alma 59:5-13
[58] See Alma 60-61
[59] Mormon 2:19 (10-19)
[60] See Mosiah 19:26, 28
[61] See Mosiah 19:29

the misunderstanding that led to the attack was sorted out and the Lamanites retreated in peace.[62] However, the Lamanite guards once again grew restless and became increasingly abusive. When the people could no longer stand being defenseless victims of the violence, they went to battle with their captors to drive them out. They took up their arms three separate times, and in each case suffered massive casualties, gained little ground, and returned home in great mourning.[63] In this deep humility, they once again subjected themselves to their captors, but also turned to God to plead for divine aid. The Lord did not grant their wishes for complete deliverance right away, but did soften the hearts of the Lamanites and their burdens became more bearable.[64] Though their circumstances were less than ideal, the people remained faithful[65] and eventually were able to escape captivity and find refuge with their fellow Nephites in Zarahemla.[66]

In just one year early in the era of Nephite judges, tens of thousands of people were killed in battles with the Lamanites.[67] The tragedy of loss of life was compounded in the following year when crops and herds that were destroyed in battle did not yield the food they needed. "*Every* soul had cause to mourn" in these perilous times; but rather than bitterness, the people chose humility, remembered their duties, repented, were baptized, and the church grew in strength. These actions resulted in "continual peace" for as long as the people remained humble.[68]

A similar pattern played out ten years later with what was then the largest battle in Nephite history. This war was centered around the people of Ammon separating themselves from the Lamanites and finding refuge among the Nephites. Their new hosts fought for them because they were under covenant obligation to not commit any more violence.

---

[62] See Mosiah 20
[63] See Mosiah 21:2-12
[64] See Mosiah 21:13-16
[65] See Mosiah 21:31-32
[66] See Mosiah 22
[67] See Alma 3:25-26
[68] See Alma 4:2-5

With the emotional climate already sweltering under these conditions, tens of thousands of Nephites and Lamanites were killed. Though the Nephites were successful in repelling the Lamanite attack, there was understandably a period of profound mourning. Prayer and fasting were notable elements of their healing process, and they were continually faithful to their covenants and obedient to the commandments. Following this period of mourning the record says, "there *began* to be continual peace."[69] Most likely, that refers to physical peace or an absence of violence. But it could also refer to peace of heart as the people were able to simultaneously acknowledge their grief and "rejoice and exult in the hope, and even know, according to the promises of the Lord" that eternal happiness awaited all the departed faithful.[70]

The Nephites were not always righteous. In just a few years after they had fought so desperately against the wicked traditions of the Lamanites, a culture of corruption, intrigue, and pride had become commonplace among the Nephites. This profound evil caused sorrow for Nephi and the Lamanites (many of whom had become more righteous as the Nephites regressed into wickedness.)[71] In both cases, we see examples of sorrow motivating positive, controllable action. The Lamanites used "every means in their power" to destroy the source of their sorrow, the proponents of wickedness.[72] Nephi saw a rapid degradation of his people, even as he diligently labored to minister to them. Wicked people had infiltrated the government and used their positions of authority to propagate evil works of every variety. In despair, he returned home from his missionary service because the people had fully rejected him.[73] He yearned to have lived in the days of his namesake when he first came to the Promised Land.[74] Though he

---

[69] Alma 30:2, emphasis added; See also Alma 28:2-6, 30:1-3
[70] Alma 28:12
[71] See Helaman 6:1-5
[72] See Helaman 6:20, 37
[73] See Helaman 7:1-3
[74] See Helaman 7:7-9; Though the Nephi of 23 B.C. yearned to live the in glorious days of Nephi of 600 B.C., we know that the earlier Nephi did not

begrudgingly accepted his lot in life that his "soul shall be filled with sorrow", he did not rest from his labors. He continued to preach repentance in the best way he could, with an apparent hope that it would turn hearts to the Savior.[75]

Over three hours in 34 A.D., the natural elements caused unfathomable destruction in the Book of Mormon lands. Storms, fires, floods, and earthquakes combined in terrible fury to destroy multiple cities (including the people in them) and even morph the local geography until it was unrecognizable.[76] When the natural violence finally subsided, a thick darkness crept in. The darkness was so potent that the people could not discern so much as a glimmer of light for three days. It is understandable, then, that these three days were filled with intense and universal mourning.[77]

Finally, the voice of Christ rang out from heaven and explained all the destruction that had occurred,[78] followed by an invitation for all survivors to repent.[79] For many hours afterwards, the people stopped mourning and sat in stunned silence.[80] After this period of silence, the voice of Christ again called the people to repentance.[81] Another wave of emotion rolled over the people, and they again mourned for all their family and friends that had been killed in the devastation.[82]

Finally, the three-day period had passed. In the morning, the sun rose, the darkness dispersed, the earth stood still, and all the scary

---

have a completely idyllic life. It is plausible to suppose the first Nephi would have been likewise eager to switch places. This is an interesting case study of how our own experiences and biases can affect our judgements of the experiences of others.

[75] See Helaman 7:4-29
[76] See 3 Nephi 8:5-19
[77] See 3 Nephi 8:20-25
[78] See 3 Nephi 9:1-12
[79] See 3 Nephi 9:13-22
[80] See 3 Nephi 10:1-2
[81] See 3 Nephi 10:3-7
[82] See 3 Nephi 10:8

noises faded into silence. In this newfound stillness in the wake of their profound trauma, the people had a choice to make. The voice of Christ had claimed responsibility for all the destruction that they had witnessed. He told them their wickedness had been the cause of the devastation. But He also promised healing, eternal life, the Holy Ghost, and refuge if they would only repent and be converted. Would they allow their hearts to grow resentful in anger towards God, or would they humbly accept the merciful invitation to come unto Christ? Inspiringly, their faith won out. Their mourning turned into joy and lamentations turned into praise and thanksgiving to Christ, "*their Redeemer.*"[83]

A CALL TO THE WORK IS A CALL TO MOURN

There are no scriptural or latter-day prophetic assurances that engaging in the Lord's work will exempt one from sorrow. Rather, scriptural evidence suggests mourning plays a vital role in ministry work and those who "take up [their] cross" [84] should expect sorrows in the work.

As one of many potential examples, consider the Jaredite prophets who mourned when their people developed hardened hearts and rejected them, so that they were forced to stop their ministry.[85]

More poignantly, Mormon prophetically promised that those "who have care for the house of Israel" *will* "sorrow for the calamity of the house of Israel…for the destruction of this people… [because they] had not repented."[86]

Mourning together in a community is an important part of becoming united in "one heart and one mind"[87] as we strive to be a Zion people.

---

[83] 3 Nephi 10:9-10, emphasis added.
[84] See Matthew 16:24-25 and 10:38-39
[85] See Ether 11:12-13
[86] Mormon 5:10-11
[87] Moses 7:18

From Alma's classic description of the baptismal covenant, we know that we must be "willing to mourn with those that mourn." In other words, anyone who has been baptized by priesthood authority is under covenant obligation to experience sorrow at times. When we join our fellow saints in mourning, comforting, and witnessing together, we are promised redemption and eternal life as part of the first resurrection.[88]

These examples illustrate that sorrow is a natural element of serving in God's kingdom. But is sorrow a byproduct of mortality that must simply be endured, or does it play a more intentional role in God's great Plan of Happiness? In other words, we *will* experience sorrow, but do we *need* to?

For insight on that question, we look again to the three Nephite disciples who wanted to remain on the earth until the Second Coming of Christ. They wanted to stay behind so that they could continue to bring souls unto Christ. The Savior worked a miracle, and their bodies underwent a kind of transfiguration where they became quasi-immortal. In this condition, they became immune to physical death and pain. They were sanctified so that Satan could not tempt them. Like angels, they are not bound by the same natural laws that we know. Apparently, they had already experienced enough physical pain, temptation, and limitations in mortality to fill the purposes of God.

However, Christ could not take away all the "bad" parts of life on earth. In the incomprehensible wisdom of God, they still needed to experience sorrow "for the sins of the world." The scriptures are silent as to explicitly explaining why this sorrow was necessary, but it seems plausible that they needed to experience this kind of sorrow if they were to be effective in their ministry of bringing souls unto Christ. When their work is finally completed, then they are promised that they will sit down in the kingdom of the Father and experience a fulness of joy, even the same joy that Christ knows.[89]

---

[88] See Mosiah 18:9 (8-11); See also Jacob 4:11
[89] See 3 Nephi 28:4-10, 13-17, 30-31, 37-40; 4 Nephi 1:44

A Man of Sorrows

As with anything else, we can look to Christ as our ultimate exemplar as we navigate our own relationship with sorrow. As the creator of all things, the ultimate source of all light and life, He "was made flesh, and dwelt among us".[90] The Son of God came to Earth so that he could suffer "pains and afflictions and temptations of every kind...[so that he could] take upon him the pains and the sicknesses of his people". He "suffered according to the flesh that he might take upon him the sins of his people, that he might blot out their transgressions according to the power of his deliverance."[91]

Isaiah poetically prophesied how the Savior would become the embodiment of grief and sorrow.[92]

> *He hath no form nor comeliness; and when we shall see him, there is no beauty that we should desire him.*
>
> *He is despised and rejected of men; a man of sorrows, and acquainted with grief: and we hid as it were our faces from him; he was despised, and we esteemed him not.*
>
> *Surely he hath borne our griefs, and carried our sorrows: yet we did esteem him stricken, smitten of God, and afflicted.*
>
> *But he was wounded for our transgressions, he was bruised for our iniquities: the chastisement of our peace was upon him; and with his stripes we are healed.*

---

[90] John 1:14 (1-4, 14)
[91] Alma 7:11-13
[92] Isaiah 53:2-5 (2-12)

Because Christ willingly suffered all these things—his complete, infinite, atoning sacrifice—he is the ultimate source of healing, comfort, and joy for all those who will come unto him.[93]

Consider this untraditional (and admittedly out-of-context) interpretation of our baptismal covenant to "mourn with those who mourn"[94]: Remember that God is one who mourns,[95] so we may think of this covenant as a direction to mourn with Him. We should mourn with Him not because He needs our comfort, but because we need the experience of mourning alongside Him. It is a parallel experience to the way you might want to "be humble with those that are humble," "love with those who love," or "forgive with those who forgive." Any godly attribute is best learned from a godly teacher. He knows what to do with sorrow and will teach you how to handle your grief. "Come unto me," He pleads to, "all ye that labour and are heavy laden." Then he promises with divine authority, "I will give you rest. Take my yoke upon you, and learn of me; for I am meek and lowly in heart: and ye shall find rest unto your souls. For my yoke is easy, and my burden is light."[96] When we mourn with God, we come closer to being like God.

As we bring our sorrows to Christ, we discover "joy because of the light of Christ unto life."[97] Alma fantasized about convincing the entire world to repent and come unto God so that sorrow would become extinct.[98] His wish was not hypothetical. That idyllic world has long been prophesied and will come when the whole earth and all its inhabitants are redeemed through the power of the atonement of Jesus Christ. Isaiah foresaw this day and prophesied "the redeemed of the Lord shall return, and come with singing unto Zion; and everlasting joy

---

[93] See 3 Nephi 9:13-15
[94] Mosiah 18:9
[95] See John 11:35, 38 (1-44), Moses 7:28 (23-40), and Isaiah 63:7-10
[96] Matthew 11:28-30
[97] Alma 28:14
[98] Alma 29:2 (1-3)

and holiness shall be upon their heads; and they shall obtain gladness and joy; sorrow and mourning shall flee away."[99]

---

[99] 2 Nephi 8:11; see also 2 Nephi 24:3 (1-8)

By Me Ye Are Led

Throughout history, God has worked with His people by leading them through perilous journeys on the way to promised lands. The golden example of such a journey is the children of Israel in Old Testament times, starting with Moses delivering his people out of Egyptian bondage and ending with Joshua leading a later generation of the same people through the Jordan River forty years later. Besides being the most well-known promised land journey, it is also the densest in terms of poignant lessons we can apply to our lives. Generations of Jews and Christians have referenced this story as a bedrock of their understanding of how God interacts with His people.[1]

Another example of God leading His people to a promised land can be found in modern times, when we look to the saga of early Latter-Day Saints first gathering at the Johnson Farm in upstate New York in April 1830, then eventually finding the "place which God for them prepared"[2] in the Salt Lake Valley in July 1847. Throughout the next half century, believers from around the world continued to flow into this Promised Land in the Intermountain region from southern Canada to northern Mexico.[3]

---

[1] See "Exodus, book of", "Joshua, book of", "Numbers", and "Wilderness of the Exodus" in the Bible Dictionary published by the Church of Jesus Christ of Latter-Day Saints.

[2] "Come, Come Ye Saints", *Hymns of the Church of Jesus Christ of Latter-Day Saints*. Deseret Book Company, Salt Lake City, Utah. 1985.

[3] See Saints: The Story of the Church of Jesus Christ in the Latter Days, Volume 1, The Standard of Truth, 1815-1846. The Church of Jesus Christ of Latter-Day Saints. Salt Lake City, Utah, 2018. and Saints: The Story of the Church of Jesus Christ in the Latter Days, Volume 2, No Unhallowed Hand, 1846-1893. The Church of Jesus Christ of Latter-Day Saints. Salt Lake City, Utah, 2020.

While these two tales are rich in history and application, limited consideration will be given to them here. Instead, this chapter will focus on two other epic tales of people being led to their respective promised lands, which are both found in the Book of Mormon. The opening chapters of the Book of Mormon tell the story of the prophet Lehi leading his family out of Jerusalem and into the Americas in 600 B.C. Later in the book, but much earlier chronologically, the Jaredites took a parallel journey from Babylon to the Americas in about 2,200 B.C.

Unlike many of the other topics in this book, this chapter is not overtly about happiness. However, a study of how God leads His people to physical promised lands can be very instructive to understanding how He may grant other blessings. The promised lands we strive for now may be a literal place—perhaps you need or want to move your family somewhere new. But there are also metaphorical promised lands that we are all pursuing. Your personal promised land may be associated with your family life, professional opportunities, health and wellbeing, discipleship, or even your pursuit of happiness. Reflect on your personal promised land as we review the stories of Lehi, Jared, and their families being led by the hand of God into the Americas.

Lehites

Lehi was one of many prophets in Jerusalem in about 600 B.C. who preached repentance and warned of impending destruction.[4] As part of his ministry, Lehi prayed "with all his heart, in behalf of his people" and consequently had an intense vision where he saw God on His throne, surrounded by angels. Christ and his apostles came to Lehi and gave him a book to read. The words of the book were a warning to Jerusalem to repent.[5]

---

[4] See 1 Nephi 1:4, 18
[5] See 1 Nephi 1:5-13

Because of this vision and other revelations Lehi received, he had great cause to praise God and rejoice.[6] However, that joy would soon be tested. When Lehi went among the people to fulfil his divinely appointed mission to testify of their wickedness, preach repentance, and prophesy of the coming Messiah, the people were offended. They were not just a little peeved and yelled at him to go away—they were angry enough to threaten his life.[7]

Having been faithful in keeping the commandments, Lehi was warned in a dream that it was time to take his family (including his wife, Sariah, and four sons) and get out of town. They gathered minimal possessions and journeyed into the wilderness. At this early stage of their journey, they may not have had a clear direction on where to travel, or even an understanding of how long they would be gone. The only certainty was that they needed to get away from a dangerous situation.[8] After three days of traveling, they set up a camp near a river. One of Lehi's first tasks in their new camp was to make an altar and give thanks to God.[9]

However, not every member of the family was filled with the same feelings of gratitude. Lehi's two oldest sons, Laman and Lemuel, complained because their dad was a visionary, which was a designation they equated with being a fool. They were also upset about leaving their material wealth behind. Most importantly, "they did murmur because they knew not the dealings of that God who had created them." Their doubtful, faithless hearts were akin to those of the people in Jerusalem who wanted to kill Lehi. Ironically, Lehi had to flee Jerusalem to escape people who wanted to kill him, but he brought two such people along on his journey—his own sons.[10] They were not entirely disobedient, though. They had willingly, if reluctantly, made the exodus with the rest of their

---

[6] See 1 Nephi 1:14-16
[7] See 1 Nephi 1:18-20
[8] See 1 Nephi 2:1-6
[9] See 1 Nephi 2:7
[10] See 1 Nephi 2:11-13

family. Their motivations for being obedient made all the difference in their attitude. In at least one episode, we know their obedience was driven by fear because of the powerful things their dad passionately told them by the Spirit.[11]

Nephi, the youngest son, had a different approach to dealing with his desires to understand his dad's decisions. He prayed to God and received a ministration that softened his heart and quenched any inclination to rebellion.[12] Because of this experience with learning truth by the Spirit, Nephi felt empowered to minister to his brothers. Sam (the third brother) believed him, but Laman and Lemuel would not. Despite his grief concerning his two oldest brothers, Nephi continued to pray to the Lord in their behalf.[13]

As part of this revelatory experience, Nephi learned parts of the Lord's long-term plans for his family. He knew he would be blessed with a promised land because of his faithfulness, while his brothers would be cut off from the Lord because of their rebellion. However, their posterity would become a bane to Nephi's posterity, with the divine purpose of keeping them motivated to remember the Lord.[14]

Not long after watching the different responses of his sons developing trust in him, Lehi had a dream that would test their faith in a very practical way. Their task, as revealed to Lehi, was to return to Jerusalem to retrieve a set of brass plates from the ruler Laban. Besides a scriptural record, these plates also included Lehi's genealogy.[15] Since they were about to cut themselves off from the rest of the house of Israel, it was imperative for them to have these records to preserve their religious and cultural identity for their posterity.[16]

---

[11] See 1 Nephi 2:14
[12] See 1 Nephi 2:16
[13] See 1 Nephi 2:17-18
[14] See 1 Nephi 2:19-24
[15] See 1 Nephi 3:2-4
[16] See 1 Nephi 3:19-20 and 5:21-22

As foreshadowed by their previously established levels of trust, Lehi's sons had diverse responses to this new commandment. Nephi's faithful response, in contrast to the murmurous response of his two oldest brothers, was a source of immense joy for Lehi. He rejoiced for Nephi because he knew that he had been and would yet be blessed by the Lord.[17]

As the four brothers made their way back to Jerusalem without their parents, they debated amongst themselves about the best way to gain possession of the brass plates.[18] Using their best ideas from their brainstorming session, they made two different attempts to get the plates, both of which failed and ended with them hiding on the outskirts of Jerusalem, penniless, tired and scared.[19] In their typical way, Laman and Lemuel grew angry and expressed their anger with physical and verbal abuse towards Nephi and Sam. The abuse ended only when an angel intervened. Besides stopping the abuse, the angel also promised that the Lord would deliver on His promises if they would only return to Jerusalem one last time.[20]

Nephi was emboldened by this divine intervention. He knew that they would be successful on their next attempt because he had faith in the Lord's promises.[21] Laman and Lemuel were affected by the angelic visit and Nephi's exhortations, but they were not overly impressed. They

---

[17] See 1 Nephi 3:8 (5-8)

[18] On their lengthy list of considerations, they may have worried about the possibility that they could be recognized as Lehi's sons, which would have added an extra element of danger to their mission.

[19] See 1 Nephi 3:9-27

[20] See 1 Nephi 3:28-30

[21] Nephi's faith in the Lord was based in part on his understanding of the scriptures. He knew the story of Moses leading the children of Israel through the Red Sea and applied it to their circumstances. This practice of comparing his experiences to what he learned in the scriptures was a notable part of Nephi's discipleship and ministry. See 1 Nephi 19:23.

went back to Jerusalem, but only with hearts full of doubt, fear, and complaint.[22]

As promised, their third attempt to retrieve the brass plates was successful. The difference this time was that Nephi was entirely dependent on the Spirit to guide him. That dependance was a necessity because he had already exhausted all his conventional wisdom. He had nowhere else to turn, so he turned to the Lord. In addition to completing the task set before him, his faith helped lead his brothers along, and to inspire one of Laban's servants, Zoram,[23] to join them in a spur-of-the-moment life altering change.[24]

Lehi and Sariah were relieved when their sons safely returned to camp, having successfully completed their assignment. The absence of their sons had been a source of intermarital stress, but also provided a space to work out their differences. By counseling with her husband through this trial, Sariah was able to strengthen her witness of the Lord's protection and enabling power.[25] The moment was significant enough that they once again offered burnt offerings for gratitude to the Lord.[26]

Lehi ensured that the sacrifices the entire family made to get the brass plates were not in vain, and at once started studying the sacred records and then prophesied concerning the things he learned. The scriptures were invaluable to him because that was how he would preserve the doctrines, commandments, and genealogies for his

---

[22] See 1 Nephi 3:31, 4:1-4

[23] Zoram was inadvertently implicated into the plot to take the brass plates out of Laban's treasury. After he discovered what was happening, he understandably became very frightened. With the power of an oath, Nephi promised Zoram life and liberty if he would stay with them. He became an integral part of the family from that time forth. See 1 Nephi 4:20-37 and 2 Nephi 1:30-32, 5:6

[24] See 1 Nephi 4:6 (4-38)

[25] See 1 Nephi 5:1-8

[26] See 1 Nephi 5:9

posterity. One of the immediate blessings he got from studying the scriptures may have been seeing the parallels between their journey and the stories of the ancient Israelites and the deliverance of Joseph of Egypt.[27]

The next episode recorded in the family's saga is when Lehi received another revelation that his sons needed to travel back to Jerusalem yet again to secure another highly valuable resource necessary for successfully establishing themselves in the Promised Land: wives. They were to visit Ishmael (likely an existing associate of the family) and convince him to bring his entire family into the wilderness and onward to the Promised Land. Though this task could have felt at least as daunting as retrieving the brass plates, there is no record of murmuring from any of Lehi and Sariah's sons on this trip back to Jerusalem. The personal payoff would have been much more tangible this time around.[28]

With the Lord's help, the brothers successfully won the hearts of Ishmael and his family and persuaded them to make the journey to the Promised Land.[29] With their prize secured, Laman and Lemuel's rebelliousness surfaced again on the journey back to Lehi and Sariah's camp. Worse than that, the unruliness and negativity infected certain members of Ishmael's family as well.[30]

Nephi responded to their protests by chiding his brothers for their faithlessness.[31] They reacted to his reprimands by tying him up and leaving him in the wilderness to be eaten by wild animals.[32] Nephi prayed in faith to be delivered from his bindings. He was freed, then stood before his brothers and spoke to them once again.[33] They did not

---

[27] See 1 Nephi 5:21 (10-22)
[28] See 1 Nephi 7:1-3
[29] See 1 Nephi 7:4-5
[30] See 1 Nephi 7:6-7
[31] See 1 Nephi 7:8-15
[32] See 1 Nephi 7:16
[33] See 1 Nephi 7:17-18

like that reversal of power. However, the intervention of three of Ishmael's family members calmed Laman and Lemuel down enough to quell their murderous ambitions. They asked for, and received, forgiveness from Nephi. He then pointed them towards God to seek His forgiveness.[34] With the latest drama behind them, both families met together in the wilderness and celebrated the momentous occasion by once again sacrificing burnt offerings in gratitude.[35]

The group seems to have stayed in this camp for a period without a clear understanding of what they were waiting for or when their time to move again would come.[36] However, we know they stayed busy. During this time, Lehi's sons and Zoram married Ishmael's daughters.[37] They gathered many seeds in preparation for a future journey and eventual settlement.[38] Lehi and Nephi both received marvelous revelations and encouraged their family to be faithful and repentant.[39] Lehi had kept all the commandments of the Lord and Nephi recognized his many blessings.[40]

Finally, their call came. In a test of their perpetual trust and sensitivity to the Spirit, the Lord spoke to Lehi in the middle of the night and directed the group to move camp deeper into the wilderness the next morning.[41]

As evidence of the divine aid they were promised, Lehi found a going away present outside his tent when he woke up to prepare to leave. It was a faith-powered compass with spindles that gave directions and changeable written messages that gave context for the divine guidance they received. The mechanics were housed in a brass ball that was

---

[34] See 1 Nephi 7:19-21
[35] See 1 Nephi 7:22
[36] See 1 Nephi 9:1
[37] See 1 Nephi 16:7
[38] See 1 Nephi 8:1
[39] See 1 Nephi 8:36-38, 16:4-5 (1-5)
[40] See 1 Nephi 16:8
[41] See 1 Nephi 16:9 (9-17, 33)

unlike anything they had ever fathomed. This Liahona, as it came to be called, inspired generations of ancient Nephites with its miraculous origin, workmanship, and power source, though it may have been less remarkable to us in the technology saturated 21st Century. However, even the most tech-savvy amongst us would have to be impressed by navigation equipment that worked only when all parties present exercised faith in Christ.[42]

As they traveled into the wilderness, they subsisted on meat they hunted along the way with bows and arrows. After many days of following the Liahona into the lushest parts of the wilderness, Nephi's bow broke. His brothers' bows were already inoperable, so the entire family was left without any means of obtaining food. Inexplicably, the focus of the brothers' hunger-fueled anger was on Nephi's broken bow and not their own bows that had become useless previously. Nevertheless, it was Nephi's problem to solve. Nephi made the best use of the materials he had available to create a new bow and arrow, then asked in faith for direction from his father. Lehi petitioned the Lord for guidance, and after some chastening for his murmuring, Lehi received the direction he needed. The Liahona directed Nephi to a mountain top where he was able to obtain sustenance for his family. As Nephi walked back into camp with his arms full of food, the family was filled with joy, humility, and gratitude to the Lord.[43]

The next major incident in their tale was the death of Ishmael. His daughters had an especially challenging time with his passing, and their grief morphed into ire towards Lehi. Two of their husbands (Laman and Lemuel), as well as their brothers, took the opportunity to stoke the fires of their ignorant anger and once again threatened to kill Lehi and Nephi. The voice of the Lord chastened them, and they repented. Consequently, the family was again blessed with food to avoid starvation.[44]

---

[42] See 1 Nephi 16:10, 16, 26-30; see also Mosiah 1:16-17 and Alma 37:38-45
[43] See 1 Nephi 16:18-26, 30-32
[44] See 1 Nephi 16:34-39

With another crisis averted, they continued their journey. Ishmael's death, with all its drama, seems to have been a turning point for the women in the group. Nephi noted how they developed improved attitudes and were as strong as the men, even as they continued to birth and nurse children. Even more extraordinary, they did so while living primarily on raw meat. The Lord had worked the miracle of making raw meat palatable and safe to keep them from building fires. These circumstances fortified Nephi's testimony that "if it so be that the children of men keep the commandments of God he doth nourish them, and strengthen them, and provide means whereby they can accomplish the thing which he has commanded them."[45]

Finally, they made it to the land Bountiful on the seashore. Bountiful received its name from its abundant wild fruit and honey. After years of surviving on raw meat, they now had wonderful new variety in their diet. They were camped on a seashore instead of wandering in a desert. This would have been a time of welcome rejuvenation for the whole group. However, the Lord prepared these things so that the Lehites could continue to *prepare* for their journey to the Promised Land. As beautiful and fertile as Bountiful was, it was only a divinely given rest stop on their way to a more ultimate blessing.[46]

The next steppingstone on their journey came when Nephi was called to go up "into the mountain." After making the trek and starting with a prayer, Nephi was instructed by the voice of God to build a ship that would carry them across the sea to their Promised Land. The call to complete this monumental task was coupled with an assurance that the Lord would show him the way. Nephi's naturally earnest and faithful attitude is reflected in his initial response to the Lord's commandment: rather than dwelling on "why" or "but…", Nephi humbly asked only to know where to find ore to make tools to make the ship.[47]

---

[45] See 1 Nephi 17:3 (1-3, 12); See also 1 Nephi 3:7
[46] See 1 Nephi 17:5-6
[47] See 1 Nephi 17:7-10

Nephi came off the mountain and went straight to work. In a very physical sense, he would need to make this ship from scratch. His first step was to make a bellows, followed by their first fire in years. He was then prepared to molten iron out of ore he had mined. Finally, he could create the tools that were necessary to build the ship.[48]

If the task of building a ship in the wilderness was not physically difficult enough, Nephi's oldest brothers took responsibility for ensuring the social and political dimensions of the project were not uncomplicated. They mocked and complained as soon as they recognized the project Nephi intended to undertake. It seems likely that their goal in murmuring was to excuse themselves from any work associated with the project. Their murmuring was a source of sorrow for Nephi, which led to them rejoicing and gloating. They supposed they would have been happier to have remained in Jerusalem with people they considered to be righteous.[49]

Their poor attitudes were a manifestation of them lacking the same vision as Nephi for finding happiness in the journey of being led by the Lord. When Nephi reprimanded his brothers for their hardened hearts and poor memories of sacred experiences, they threatened to throw him into the sea. Nephi asserted his confidence in divine protection and aid. Much less than tossing him off a cliff, they found they could not so much as lay a finger on him for several days. They eventually had enough strong exposure to the Spirit of God, with Nephi acting as the conduit, that they found the humility to repent.[50]

Their penitence finally allowed the whole group of brothers to work together as a cohesive team to complete the monumental task before them. The way they built the ship was after the Lord's pattern, and not their own. The plans for the ship were given to Nephi incrementally as he went to the mountain often to pray and receive revelation. When the

---

[48] See 1 Nephi 17:11,16
[49] See 1 Nephi 17:17-22
[50] See 1 Nephi 17:44-55 (23-55)

job was completed, they all marveled at the work they had completed and humbled themselves once more before the Lord.[51]

With the ship ready to sail, the last remaining task was to load it with provisions they had prepared. This period would have been a high point for Lehi and Sariah's family. As far as we can tell from the recorded history, apart from the drama of getting Laman and Lemuel on board with the project, they had all worked together from mining the first lump of ore to loading the last seed. With unified and faith-filled hearts, they launched themselves into the sea and let the winds drive them towards the Promised Land.[52]

Unfortunately, it was a short-lived phase. After several days at sea, several members of the family used their newly rediscovered free time to get carried into idleness, which spiraled into rudeness and then forgetfulness. Sensing impending danger, Nephi tried to talk some reason into them, but it did not work. Their angry, jealous response was to bind Nephi's hands and feet and abuse him. For four days, the Lord caused a storm to rage which blew them off course. Furthermore, their worldliness had cut off the power source of the Liahona,[53] and it stopped functioning. The abusers threatened anyone who spoke on Nephi's behalf. Only the fear of being dashed apart by the waves was enough motivation to soften their hearts enough to remove Nephi's bindings. With swollen wrists and ankles, Nephi held the Liahona, and it miraculously began to work again. He then offered a prayer and the storm subsided. With peace restored to the family and the sea, they were able to sail safely once more.[54]

After setting foot on solid ground, they began to till and cultivate it. They planted the seeds they had prepared in the wilderness, and the crops thrived in the fertile ground. They found many animals in the forests that they could make practical use of for meat and for

---

[51] See 1 Nephi 18:1-4
[52] See 1 Nephi 18:5-6, 8
[53] See 1 Nephi 16:28
[54] See 1 Nephi 18:9-22

domestication. They also discovered various kinds of ore that would be useful for civilization. Though it was an unfamiliar environment, their resource-rich new home would have stood out in stark contrast to the desert home they left in Jerusalem. It would have been easy to regard it as the Promised Land they were anticipating.[55]

However, it was yet again a fleeting experience, and it was not yet the Promised Land the Lord had prepared for Nephi and those that would follow him. Though the land may have been idyllic, the social environment was not. Despite all the miracles they had experienced, Nephi's brothers had still not found lasting change in their hearts and once again wanted to kill him.[56] Consequently, Nephi had to leave what he may have *thought* was his promised land for the sake of his personal safety. He took a group of those that believed him and traveled many days further inland and once again built a new civilization in righteousness and gratitude.[57] Here, they were finally able to make a permanent home and "live after the manner of happiness."[58]

JAREDITES

Everything we know about the Jaredites comes from an abridgement that Moroni made of twenty-four gold plates that were found by the people of Limhi in about 121 B.C. We know Moroni's abridgement of this record as the Book of Ether, which gives the entire 2,100-year history of this people. We also know that Moroni did not cover all twenty-four plates in his abridgement because the first part of the record was the story of the creation of the world down to the tower of Babel, and Moroni supposed that history was recorded sufficiently elsewhere.[59]

---

[55] See 1 Nephi 18:23-25
[56] See 2 Nephi 5:1-7
[57] See 2 Nephi 5: 8-19, 27
[58] 2 Nephi 5:27
[59] Ether 1:1-5; see also Mosiah 21:27, 28:11-12, 17

Thus, we know relatively little about the history of the Jaredites, but the details we do have are inspiring.

The story of the Jaredites starts at the tower of Babel when the people were so wicked that the Lord had to confound their language and scatter them. Being an exception to the crowd, Jared was a righteous man, and he led a group of people away from Babylon for physical, social, and spiritual safety.[60]

Jared seems to have been dependent on his brother for communion with the Lord. Specifically, Jared asked that his brother pray to the Lord for protection three distinct times: once for their own safety, once on behalf of their friends, and once to know if the Lord would lead them to a "land which is choice above all the earth." In each case the Lord answered with compassion and granted the request.[61]

In response to the request to inherit a promised land, the Lord assured them He would lead them out of Babylon to a special land and there make them a great nation—the greatest on the face of the earth. But before that could happen, they had to first gather their flocks, seeds, families, and friends, and then make a journey to a specific valley. Only then did the Lord promise to meet them and start their journey to the Promised Land.[62]

Their land of promise would be superior to all other lands and had been preserved for a righteous people. Because the land was so special, part of the terms of their agreement were that they could stay only as long they and their descendants continued to serve the Lord. However, the Lord would withhold His wrath "until the fulness of iniquity among the children of the land."[63]

---

[60] See Ether 1:33
[61] See Ether 1:34-40
[62] See Ether 1:40-43
[63] See Ether 2:10 (7-12); This promise from the Lord is one reason why Moroni emphatically pleaded with the inheritors of the Promised Land to continue to serve the God of the land, who is Jesus Christ.

When they had prepared themselves as commanded, the Lord met them in the valley as He had committed. He spoke to the brother of Jared from a cloud but remained veiled. He stayed in a cloud as He traveled ahead of them, guiding them along the way. They were directed to travel into a part of the wilderness that had never been seen by human eyes.[64]

The wilderness they were traveling in was filled with bodies of water big enough they could not simply walk through or around. They learned to traverse these obstacles by building barges to load themselves, their animals, and provisions and then float across. We can assume they would have had to make new barges every time they came to a new impassable water body because it is unlikely that they could have portaged vessels large enough to carry everyone and everything. As they crossed one water body after another, they knew they would eventually cross the ocean before inheriting the Promised Land. Hopefully, they conscientiously learned from each water crossing and viewed it as practice for their impending ocean voyage.[65]

The Lord led the Jaredites to the seashore, where they set up camp and stayed for a while. After four years, the Lord again visited the brother of Jared in a cloud. For three hours, the Lord chastised him because he had forgotten to pray to Him during this time. The brother of Jared repented, and the Lord forgave him. However, his forgiveness came with a stern reminder that His Spirit is not a guaranteed companion. If anyone fails to repent, they will continue in sin until they are "fully ripe" and qualify to be cut off from the Lord. Being repentant and trusting in the Spirit was a qualification for inheriting the Promised Land.[66]

Granting forgiveness for their slothfulness, the Lord told them to get to work building more barges according to His instructions, just like the ones they had been taught to build in the wilderness. The whole group

---

[64] See Ether 2:1, 4-5
[65] See Ether 2:6-7
[66] See Ether 2:13-15

worked together to build this last set of eight small, light, and impermeable vessels. The brother of Jared then reported back to the Lord that they had completed the task.[67]

Though the barges were built well, the brother of Jared saw two major drawbacks with the design: being so watertight also meant they were airtight and light tight. That would make for a long, stifling, dark journey. So, he problem solved with the Lord—the designer of the barges—about how to ensure they would have fresh air and light during their voyage.

This was not a design oversight like most engineers might be susceptible to. In His infinite wisdom, the Lord knew air and light would be necessary, and He knew how to resolve the issues. Rather than a conversation between an engineer and contractor, this was a conversation between teacher and student. The Lord used this experience to help the brother of Jared build the confidence to solve his own problems.

The Lord gave a direct answer when asked about fresh air but was more nuanced about the issue of light. He counseled with the brother of Jared to help him find his own solution to the problem, but still freely offered His divine aid.[68] The brother of Jared humbly offered his best effort to the Lord, and the Lord worked a miracle to provide a light source for the Jaredites.[69]

Because of the faith he developed while problem solving the issue of light, the brother of Jared was able to have a remarkable revelation where he saw the premortal Christ and all the inhabitants of the earth. He learned directly from the Master Teacher about redemption, the divinity of Christ, creation of body and spirit, and the relationship between faith and knowledge.[70]

---

[67] See Ether 2:16 (16-18)
[68] See Ether 2:19-25
[69] See Ether 3:1-6, 6:2-3
[70] See Ether 3:7-26

With the barges prepared, the people continued to work diligently as they prepared all necessary supplies for their voyage of an unknown duration. Stepping onto their barges was a tremendous act of faith because they had no means of control. They were entirely dependent on the Lord to power and steer their vessels to wherever He wanted them to go. They could not have even guaranteed that the group of barges would stay together during their voyage. It would be understandable if they had worried about the possibility of never again seeing the people in the other barges.[71]

The Lord powered them towards the Promised Land with "furious wind" and "mountain waves" for 344 days. When they were submerged for too long, they would pray with faith and the Lord would bring them once again to the surface. We do not know how stable the vessels were, but we can be confident it was a wild ride with livestock, supplies, and people being continually bumped around in a confined space. Nevertheless, they sang ceaseless praises to the Lord.[72]

When their feet were finally again on solid ground, they dropped to their knees and offered tearful, humble praise to the Lord for the many miracles they had experienced on their journey.[73] They then stood up and got to work building a new civilization.[74] They prospered, in part because "they were taught to walk humbly before the Lord; and they were also taught from on high."[75]

Promise Lands

Studying historical examples of God leading people to promised lands in the context of modern-day experiences can be richly instructive to understand how God works with His children. Though you may be

---

[71] See Ether 6:4
[72] See Ether 6:5-11
[73] See Ether 6:12
[74] See Ether 6:13
[75] Ether 6:17 (17-18)

familiar with the stories we have reviewed here, they can take on new vibrancy as you discover parallels between them and your life experience, just like Nephi and Lehi did with the story of the ancient Israelites. One of the starkest lessons we can learn from these peoples being led to their promised land was that neither the journey nor the destination was ever care-free or easy.

Focusing on the richness of a promised land "flowing with milk and honey"[76] can easily lead to a false concept of God's true purposes in leading His people on a such a journey. It is more instructive to instead think about *Promise* Lands—lands where we can learn about the promises God has made to us. Those who "trust in the Lord with all [their] heart"[77] to guide their lives often find that their hope is rooted entirely in the promises made by the Lord through revelation and covenants. When it seems all mortal efforts are in vain, faith in the Lord's promises becomes an enabling power to continue to wait patiently.

Nephi had faith in the Lord's commandments from the time his family left Jerusalem,[78] but the experiences he had on the journey to his Promised Land strengthened his testimony of obedience. After discussing the miracle of thriving on raw meat, he reflected "If it so be that the children of men keep the commandments of God he doth nourish them, and strengthen them, and provide means whereby they can accomplish the thing which he has commanded them."[79] Soon after this testimony, the Lord directly promised His divine guidance and aid to Nephi, then reminded him, "Inasmuch as ye shall keep my commandments ye shall be led towards the promised land; and *ye shall know that it is by me that ye are led.*" He then prophetically promised,

---

[76] Exodus 3:8
[77] Proverbs 3:5
[78] See 1 Nephi 3:7
[79] 1 Nephi 17:3

"*after ye have arrived in the promised land, ye shall know that I, the Lord, am God.*"[80]

One of the primary purposes of this journey from Jerusalem to the Americas was so that they could know indisputably that the Lord had delivered them. They saw so many miracles along the way that there was no other plausible explanation than divine care and intervention. For Nephi (but not everyone in the family), the gratitude and wonderment he felt towards the Lord's blessings led to natural strivings for greater obedience and to encourage his family to be likewise faithful. He came to know God in the wilderness because that is where God made and fulfilled His holy promises.[81]

ROADMAP TO YOUR PERSONAL PROMISED LAND

Promised lands are for righteous people because it takes wholehearted discipleship to get there. There are no scriptural examples of righteous people being air-dropped into their Promised Land as soon as they earned their great reward elsewhere. In every case, the Lord started with a people living in less-than-ideal circumstances and then miraculously led them through an even more difficult wilderness. On their journey, they were refined through adversity and fidelity. Only then were they qualified to inherit the special lands that God had reserved for a special people.

If we are seeking special blessings from God—righteous, divinely-compatible desires of our hearts—we can expect that the Lord will grant

---

[80] 1 Nephi 17:13-14, emphasis added; Note the symbol of the Lord being their light in the wilderness as an added manifestation of the divine aid they were promised. This light source was powered by obedience.

[81] See 2 Nephi 4:20 (19-25) and 1 Nephi 17:15; Though Laman and Lemuel were on the same physical journey as Nephi, their spiritual journey was vastly different. Consequently, there is no evidence that they were being led towards a promised land. Because they refused to learn about the promises of the Lord, they were not promised His blessings.

a way to receive those blessings in His own time and way. However, we should not expect any less of a toilsome journey than what we learn about in the scriptures. The major benefit we have over the Israelites, Jaredites, Lehites, and latter-day pioneers, is that we have their experiences as proven history to know how God works. They were trailblazers, and we can now use their experiences as a roadmap to our personal promised lands. Consider how the following lessons from the Lehites and Jaredites may apply to your pursuit of happiness or another personal promised land.

Focus on Positivity

One of Nephi's purposes in making his record was to testify of the miracles his family saw because of their faith.[82] As one example, it would have been understandable if he had lamented subsisting on raw meat for years on end. Instead, he chose to marvel at the miracle of thriving while the Lord made their meat palatable and safe without the use of fire.[83]

Lehi was exceptional at leading his family in offering burnt offerings of gratitude at key points in their journey. He did it when they first left Jerusalem,[84] when his sons returned with the brass plates,[85] and when Ishmael's family joined them.[86] Their gratitude was coupled with humility and joy when Nephi returned to camp with the food he hunted with his improvised bow and arrow. [87]

Similarly, the Jaredites offered tearful praise to God "because of the multitude of his tender mercies over them" when their voyage was over.[88] This worship was in addition to the continual praises they sang

---

[82] See 1 Nephi 1:20
[83] See 1 Nephi 17:3 (1-3, 12)
[84] See 1 Nephi 2:6-7
[85] See 1 Nephi 5:9
[86] See 1 Nephi 7:22
[87] See 1 Nephi 16:32
[88] See Ether 6:12

as they were bumped, rolled, and thrown towards the Promised Land in their barges. For the Jaredites, the miracle of safety and the assurance of better things to come was greater than any discomfort they might have felt.[89] The example of both groups focusing on the positive aspects of their journey is enlightening for all of us.

There are images circulating around the internet that are used to make a point about the natural-man tendency to focus on negative things; you may have seen one such image. The image I am picturing features thousands of big, bright yellow flowers in a field. This field expands into a background of a snowcapped alpine mountain range reaching up into a crystal blue sky with fluffy white clouds. In the center foreground is a single, dead flower. When asked what they first notice about the picture, many people ignore the carpet of yellow, the majestic mountains, and beautiful sky. Instead, they are quick to point out the single flaw: the dead flower.

Ignoring difficulties will not always make them vanish, but fixating on them will be even less helpful. Being wise with your limited energy and resources can help you make the best of any situation. Intentional positivity and gratitude are not about ignoring the reality of your troubles. They are about making the best of a situation so that you can maximize your emotional capacity to face your problems and address them with greater clarity.

MINISTER TO OTHERS

The road to the Promised Land is not meant to be walked alone. Lehi and Jared took their families with them, but they invited others as well. "It was not meet for [Lehi to] take his family into the wilderness alone," primarily because his sons needed wives to start families.[90] We may infer added reasoning that is not documented. For instance, Ishmael must have been at least an acquaintance (if not a friend) of Lehi's. We can be certain he was not in the mob that drove Lehi out of Jerusalem

---

[89] See Ether 6:9 (5-11)
[90] 1 Nephi 7:1 (1-5)

but was more likely of the same caliber in terms of obedience to the Lord. His life may very well have needed to be preserved in the same way and for the same reasons as Lehi's, and the sons of Lehi were the Lord's hands in extending mercy to Ishmael's family.

When Jared and his brother saw the impending destruction at Babylon, their thoughts went first to the protection of their own families and then, charitably, to their friends. Like Lehi, the Lord compassionately allowed them to invite their friends' families so that they may likewise be saved from destruction and inherit the Promised Land.[91]

Part of ministering to others is bearing testimony. Nephi and Lehi were both admirable in this practice. Nephi frequently and fervently taught his brothers the commandments and encouraged them to be faithful. Sometimes, his brothers would respond to the Spirit and humbly repent. When they did, Nephi rejoiced and continued to hope wonderful things for them.[92]

In his final days of mortality, having lived to inherit the Promised Land, Lehi gathered his posterity and rehearsed their deliverance story to them. He testified of the Lord's mercies in saving their lives from the wicked people in Jerusalem, as well as the consequences of their own rebellions. He bore witness of the Lord's blessings and miracles, despite all the difficulties they faced along the way. Elder Neil L. Andersen would call this a "spiritually defining memory" for Lehi, and he used it to help light the path his posterity would continue to walk after he was gone.[93]

Nephi also looked beyond his own generation for opportunities to minister to others. One of his purposes in keeping his records was to persuade people to come unto Christ and be saved.[94] He was very

---

[91] See Ether 1:36-37 (33-42)
[92] For example, see 1 Nephi 15:2-11 and 16:4-5 (1-5)
[93] See 2 Nephi 1:1-5; see also Neil L. Andersen, "Spiritually Defining Memories", *Liahona*, May 2020, 18-22.
[94] See 1 Nephi 6:4

intentional with every stroke he engraved. In the part of his story right after they arrived in the Promised Land, he said, "I do not write anything upon plates save it be that I think it to be sacred."[95] He was not blogging for a travel site or sadfishing on social media; his purpose was much more celestial than seeking worldly attention and praise. He saw the eternal value in the things he went through—positive and negative— on his promised land journey. He experienced a whole-hearted conversion to the Lord, and the natural consequence of such a transformation is an overwhelming desire to share the experience with others. Every detail we know about Nephi's story is a sacred memory of his, in which he saw enduring value for future generations as they faced their own challenges in coming to know God. That desire to be a guide for anyone along the way, whether they be near or far, is the essence of true ministering.

Seek and Receive Personal Revelation

In April 2018, President Russel M. Nelson fervently pleaded for each member of the Church to grow in their capacity to receive personal revelation and boldly warned, "In coming days, it will not be possible to survive spiritually without the guiding, directing, comforting, and constant influence of the Holy Ghost."[96]

Each member of Lehi's family had to reach a personal understanding of the reality of his prophetic mission. Such a witness could only come by revelation. In their first days out of Jerusalem, Laman and Lemuel complained "because they knew not the dealings of that God who had created them."[97] In contrast, Nephi's "great desires to know the mysteries of God" led him to humble prayer, which resulted in a visit from the Lord, a softened heart, and faith in the words of his father. Because of those things, Nephi had no desire to rebel like his brothers

---

[95] 1 Nephi 19:6 (6-7)
[96] Russell M. Nelson, "Revelation for the Church, Revelation for Our Lives", *Liahona,* May 2018, 93-96.
[97] 1 Nephi 2:12 (12-13)

did.[98] This simple experience with revelation at an early age set him up for a lifetime of humble, devoted, and miracle-rich discipleship. It was the beginning of a lifetime practice of seeking revelation, which was key to his physical and spiritual survival.

For example, Nephi's efforts to obtain the brass plates were successful only when he allowed himself to be "led by the Spirit, not knowing beforehand the things which [he] should do." It was difficult and uncomfortable, but his reliance on the Spirit allowed him to do the work God had asked him to do.[99] This experience with the brass plates was another steppingstone in preparation for later trials of faith that he would face.

We do not know about Nephi's experience with blacksmithing, carpentry, and related crafts while growing up in Jerusalem. He may have had some familiarity with working with his hands; nevertheless, it is highly likely that the Lord's command to build a ship would have seemed an unfathomably unfamiliar, large, and arduous task. Nephi's self-assessment of the finished product was that it was "good, and that the workmanship thereof was exceedingly fine." How did Nephi become an expert shipbuilder? He relied on the Lord for frequent, incremental revelation. He often went into the mountains, where he prayed and was shown "great things." When he had received a bit of the Lord's word on shipbuilding, he left the mountain and went to work with his brothers until he needed further direction. The product was the Lord's ship—not a ship that was built according to mortal understanding.[100]

Nephi had an incredibly rich revelatory experience when he received the vision of the tree of life and then prophetically saw the full history of the Promised Land, including the destruction of his people and the eventual end of the world. After seeing so many great and terrible things, Nephi was physically and emotionally exhausted. His grief was compounded when he returned to camp to find his brothers once again

---

[98] See 1 Nephi 2:16 (16-24).
[99] See 1 Nephi 4:6 (4-38).
[100] See 1 Nephi 18:1-4

arguing about Lehi's teachings. One of their points of contention was a persistent belief that the Lord would not help them understand difficult subjects. Their words fell hollow on Nephi's ears because of his personal witness to the remarkable things the Lord is eager to share with His children. Nephi knew, indisputably, that the key to revelation is obedience to the commandments, softening your heart, and asking the Lord in faith.[101]

Lehi's entire family learned principles of revelation when they were gifted the Liahona. They learned through their experience with this divine object that heavenly direction was available only when they unitedly exercised faith in and obedience to God's word.[102]

Like Nephi, the brother of Jared had a remarkable experience with learning the shipbuilding trade by revelation. The description given of the Jaredite barges is unlike any conventional understanding of proper shipbuilding practice—these were the Lord's barges. Unlike Nephi, though, the Jaredites built several sets of barges during their journey through the wilderness. The Lord generously allowed them to practice on lower-stakes water crossings before they prepared to cross the ocean. When they built the last set of barges, they were able to do so with minimal specific direction. However, the issue of having enough air and light on such a long voyage was a new challenge they had to address.[103]

---

[101] See 1 Nephi 15:11 (2-11)

[102] See 1 Nephi 16:28 (26-32) and 18:12-13, 20-22; It is especially interesting to note that when Nephi inquired where to find food to support his family, the Liahona led him onto a mountain top. Similarly, Nephi became a ship builder by receiving revelation in the mountains. We can likewise find plentiful spiritual nourishment for our families and other unconventional wisdom in the Mountain of the Lord—the temple.

The symbolism of the Liahona being a guide for us to follow the words of Christ into our own land of promise was explained centuries later by one of Lehi's descendants, Alma. See Alma 37:43-45 (38-45)

[103] See Ether 2:16-19; See also 1 Nephi 18:2

The Lord gave a direct answer to the brother of Jared on how to solve the issue of having enough air in these otherwise impenetrable vessels.[104] Conversely, He was much more nuanced in helping the brother of Jared discover how to solve the problem of light. They counseled together about the issue and potential solutions that would not work. The Lord was unwavering in offering His divine support, but it was up to the brother of Jared to propose a solution for light. He humbly offered up his best effort and the Lord magnified it in a miraculous way. [105]

If you are to enroll yourself in the school of personal revelation, you must learn to pray more humbly and sincerely. You need to search the scriptures with greater intent and find ways to apply the stories and doctrines to your personal circumstances.[106] You would do well to be more conscientious in living to be worthy of the constant companionship of the Holy Ghost through obedience and personal purity. You will come to understand more deeply the importance of acting in faith on revelation you have received. Through these efforts, you will grow in your ability to discern the voice of the Spirit from other thoughts and influences.

As promised in the scriptures, revelation most often comes "line upon line...here a little and there a little."[107] Revelation may sometimes come as an unexpected thought, and other times after an extended period of study and prayer. Occasionally, the revelation may be an

---

[104] See Ether 2:20-21

[105] See Ether 2:22-25, 3:1-6, and 6:2-3; See also Genesis 6:16, footnote a. Several gospel teachers have observed it is possible that the reason the Lord did not give a direct answer on how to light the interior of a vessel is that He had already solved that problem for Noah. The task for the brother of Jared was not to produce a solution out of thin air, but to go search his scriptures to see what the Lord had previously done for His children.

[106] Nephi was especially good at applying the scriptures to his circumstances. See 1 Nephi 17: 23-42, 50-51 for one example of when he drew on the stories of the ancient Israelites to make sense of his own experiences.

[107] 2 Nephi 28:30

articulate voice giving directions on your next step, yet other times, it may be a general feeling of comfort that "all things [will] work together for [your] good."[108] As you intentionally learn to discern the many voices of the Spirit, you will develop a confidence that each revelation is a timely message from your loving Father in Heaven.

Your life may feel chaotic and your future uncertain, but as you lean into your personal revelation, you will find "the peace of God, which passeth all understanding".[109] You will discover that the peace that grows out of individualized divine communication is greater than the understanding of conventional logic, limited perspective, and naive desires. Moreover, you will find added peace in heeding President Nelson's prophetic warning to grow in your ability to receive personal revelation. You will be able to echo his testimony that personal revelation is "one of the greatest gifts of God to His children."[110]

USE AGENCY RIGHTEOUSLY

As part of his final teachings to his family, Lehi taught Jacob about the necessary use of agency in mortality.[111] Elder David A. Bednar expounded on Lehi's teachings in the context of responding to difficult social interactions:

> *In the grand division of all of God's creations, there are things to act and things to be acted upon. As sons and daughters of our Heavenly Father, we have been blessed with the gift of moral agency, the capacity for independent action and choice. Endowed with agency, you and I are agents, and we primarily are to act and not just be acted upon. To believe that someone or something can make us feel offended, angry, hurt, or*

---

[108] Romans 8:28
[109] Philippians 4:7
[110] Russell M. Nelson, "Revelation for the Church, Revelation for Our Lives", *Liahona,* May 2018, 93-96.
[111] See 2 Nephi 2:14 (11-16)

bitter diminishes our moral agency and transforms us into objects to be acted upon. As agents, however, you and I have the power to act and to choose how we will respond to an offensive or hurtful situation.[112]

The use of moral agency by God's children was one of the critical issues at stake in the War in Heaven. Lucifer became Satan because he rejected that divine gift. When he fell, he took one third of God's spirit children with him. Every effort of the Adversary and his minions since that time has been directed towards usurping the Father's glory and limiting our agency. Though we can be assured of his ultimate demise, he has been successful in claiming many more casualties in his traps.[113] Every cord of bondage that Satan wraps around one of God's children thwarts God's work and robs His glory.[114]

The gift of moral agency for humankind has come at an enormous cost for the Father of Heaven and Earth. It would be the height of hypocrisy for Him to compel us into any divine blessing. Any time you feel coerced into an action—even a "good" one—it should be a cue to stop, consider the source of your motivations, and honestly evaluate your complete list of options with their attendant consequences. When your assessment is complete, you can go on with making faith-filled use of your God-given agency in the way that He intended.

Nephi completed this exercise with his brothers when he reminded them that they had a choice in leaving Jerusalem. He left open the option for them to return home but prophesied that going back would lead to their demise.[115]

---

[112] David A. Bednar, "And Nothing Shall Offend Them", *Ensign,* November 2006, 89-91.

[113] See Moses 4:3(1-4), Doctrine and Covenants 29:35-39, and Isaiah 14:12-14 (12-17)

[114] See Moses 1:39

[115] See 1 Nephi 7:15 (7, 13-15)

Nephi repeatedly made exemplary decisions as he helped his family towards the Promised Land. When his family was left without any functioning weapons to hunt for food, Nephi avoided the tendency to lay blame on others or to dwell on the precariousness of their situation. Instead, he focused on the one thing he *could* do. He crafted a new bow and arrow, inferior to his old bow and arrow as they were, and then sought the Lord's help to know the best place to use them. [116]

His humility was on display again as he was tasked with building a ship in the wilderness. When the monumental task was set before him, he could have had a range of reactions, most of them negative—disbelief, disgust, helplessness, hopelessness, etc. Instead, he chose faith. He started with the most basic first step in shipbuilding—finding ore to make tools—and then faithfully persisted until the job was complete.[117]

Throughout their journey, Nephi and Lehi gained many witnesses of the connection between faithfulness and blessings. On the return trip from gathering Ishmael's family, Laman and Lemuel began to grow rebellious. In his response to them, Nephi emphasized his testimony that the Lord can do all things for His children when they *exercise* faith in Him. That testimony was anchored in his vivid memories of the miracles he had seen in obtaining the brass plates.[118]

In reflecting on the miracle of thriving on raw meat, Nephi bore his testimony of God's blessings for keeping the commandments. For Nephi, those blessings included nourishment, strength, and enabling power to fulfill God's commandments.[119] The promise of nourishment and strength in exchange for obedience applied in a physical sense for Nephi's family, but it also applies in a spiritual sense for all of us. Another name for the enabling power that Nephi experienced is grace. Paul's declaration to the Philippians would have resonated with Nephi,

---

[116] See 1 Nephi 16:18-26, 30-32
[117] See 1 Nephi 17:7-18, 49-55, 18:1-6, 8
[118] See 1 Nephi 7:12-13 (8-15)
[119] See 1 Nephi 17:3

"I can do all things through Christ which strengtheneth me."[120] It is by grace that all those who receive Christ are promised to receive of His fulness.[121]

Returning to Lehi's final teachings to his posterity, we read how he emphatically taught that the Promised Land is for those who keep the covenants of the Lord. The Promised Land was, and is, a land of liberty free from oppression from others. This promise applied not only to the first generation who fled Jerusalem, but to their descendants and anyone else from other countries who would be led to the Promised Land by the Lord. The only condition that can violate this covenant is when those who inherit the land use their agency to do wickedness.[122]

WAIT ON THE LORD

As the Jaredite barges were nearing completion, the brother of Jared recognized the potential problem of not having light inside of them. Naturally, he approached the Lord to ask for divine help in solving this problem. The Lord's response to this specific question was to remind him of all the things He had already prepared for the Jaredites. He then turned the tables back to the brother of Jared, asking him what his recommendation would be to light the interior of the barges.[123]

The brother of Jared set to work by creating sixteen small, transparent stones. He then took these stones—representing his best mortal effort—before the Lord and asked Him to sanctify them. He went with confidence, knowing he was keeping the commandment to call upon the Lord for divine aid. With extreme humility, he pleaded for mercy and asked the Lord to touch the stones and make them glow with

---

[120] Philippians 4:13
[121] See John 1:12-17; see also John 15:1-11, Ephesians 2:8-9, 2 Nephi 25:23, and Moroni 10:32-32
[122] See 2 Nephi 1:5, 7 (5-11); see also 2 Nephi 4:4
[123] See Ether 2:22-25

divine power. The Lord responded to his complete trust and reached out His finger.[124]

The original issue at stake was to ask for help with making the stones glow, and that goal was completed. However, the brother of Jared had much more of a divine encounter than he could have ever expected. This experience included a personal ministration from the premortal Christ, a promise of redemption and exaltation, a commandment to write about his experience in an unknown language (plus a Urim and Thummim by which a future seer would interpret his writings[125]), and a vision of every mortal that ever had and ever would live on the earth. This miraculous revelatory experience happened for two reasons: one, his faith had matured into knowledge, and he could no longer be kept from outside the veil; and two, so that he could know that the Lord is God and then testify to others.[126]

This episode of the brother of Jared trusting in the Lord's miracles to provide light inside the barges exemplifies teachings from Elder Robert D. Hales:

> "The purpose of our life on earth is to grow, develop, and be strengthened through our own experiences. How do we do this? The scriptures give us an answer in one simple phrase: we "wait upon the Lord." Tests and trials are given to all of us. These mortal challenges allow us and our Heavenly Father to see whether we will exercise our agency to follow His Son. He already knows, and we have the opportunity to learn, that no matter how difficult our circumstances, "all these things shall [be for our] experience, and ... [our] good."

---

[124] See Ether 3:5 (3:1-6, 6:2-3)
[125] See Mosiah 8:13-18 and Doctrine and Covenants 17:1
[126] See Ether 3:26-27 (6-28)

> "...What, then, does it mean to wait upon the Lord? In the scriptures, the word wait means to hope, to anticipate, and to trust. To hope and trust in the Lord requires faith, patience, humility, meekness, long-suffering, keeping the commandments, and enduring to the end."[127]

Sariah learned this lesson when she had the excruciating task of waiting for her sons to return from Jerusalem. She found comfort while waiting by counseling with Lehi and hearing his witness of the Lord's promises. When her sons returned, having been successful in their mission, she gained a stronger testimony of Lehi's call and of the Lord's power. It was critical that she gained this witness early in their journey. As the matriarch of this family with many difficult years ahead, she needed full reservoirs of faith and hope at the onset.[128]

Nephi chose to allow his faith to be greater than his fear. In the first days after leaving Jerusalem, the Lord blessed him for his faithfulness, diligence, and meekness. His promised blessing was that he would be led to a Promised Land, which was prepared for *him*. That blessing came after he had chosen to ask in faith for a witness of his dad's mission, rather than succumbing to the fear-based anger his brothers had espoused.[129]

Nephi's faith-filled attitude helped him see beyond all the fears he potentially faced and trust the Lord to fulfill His promises. One of his major sources of inspiration was his understanding of the story of Moses leading the Israelites through the Red Sea. As we follow Nephi's example and deepen our own understanding of the scriptures, we can

---

[127] Robert D. Hales, "Waiting upon the Lord: Thy Will Be Done", Ensign, November 2011, 71-73. See also Isaiah 40:31 and Doctrine and Covenants 122:7

[128] See 1 Nephi 5:8 (1-9)

[129] See 1 Nephi 2:19-20 (16-24)

likewise know how God has worked with His people in the past and gain confidence in how He will work with us.[130]

A cornerstone of Lehi's foundation of faith was an understanding that God's plan was bigger than himself. It was this assurance that enabled Lehi to wait on the Lord through all his afflictions. For example, the Lord blessed Lehi for fulfilling his prophetic mission. The blessing for his faithfulness was being led away from his home and wealth, into the wilderness towards the Promised Land. While difficult to bear, his exodus from Jerusalem saved his life.[131]

Lehi knew his family's place in the Lord's plan. By being led into a promised land in the Americas, they were fulfilling the Lord's word that Israel would be scattered to the whole earth. That scattering was necessary so that Israel could be gathered again in the latter days, giving all people of the earth an opportunity to come to know the true Messiah. While it saved their lives, their exodus fulfilled a purpose much larger than the concerns of their immediate family.[132]

Nephi also knew that the full blessings of the Lord would not come for generations. He had a vision of the Promised Land where he saw masses of people fighting wars with each other. Generations passed, and then he saw darkness, storms, earthquakes, and destruction of entire cities. Then, after all this destruction, Nephi saw the glorious ministry of Christ among his people.[133] After Christ's ministry, Nephi saw that the descendants of his brothers would eventually conquer his posterity. The Lamanites would go on to spread over the whole land and "dwindle in unbelief" and become very wicked.[134]

Later in his life, Nephi prophesied of the day when his father's posterity would once again be brought to a remembrance of their fathers, their connection to the house of Israel, and a knowledge of Jesus

---

[130] See 1 Nephi 4:1-3
[131] See 1 Nephi 2:1-4
[132] See 1 Nephi 10:13 (12-14)
[133] See 1 Nephi 12:1-6
[134] See 1 Nephi 12:14-15, 19-23

Christ. This knowledge would become a reason for rejoicing as they once again become a "pure and a delightsome people."[135] In other words, Nephi knew that many generations would separate his journey to the Promised Land, and the complete fulfillment of the Lord's promises to his posterity.

Nephi had a proven faith in the Lord's foreknowledge and ability to fulfill His promises. This testimony compelled him to make the significant effort to engrave two sets of plates. He knew the Lord had commanded it but did not know why.[136] With our modern-day perspective, we can see how two sets of records were necessary to preserve his words and thus facilitate the future redemption of his people.[137]

There is a bit of irony in Nephi simultaneously:

(1) Knowing that his father's posterity would eventually come to know their Redeemer in the Promised Land.
(2) Knowing that the Lord had requested two sets of records.
(3) Not realizing that it was his own sacrifices—millennia in advance—that would enable the fulfillment of God's promises in the latter days.

This experience underscores the critical need to completely trust the Lord in all things because we cannot foresee the miraculous chain of events that our current obedience and sacrifices will set in motion. God's plan is far too great, far too glorious for our mortal minds to grasp. However, we each can trust Him day by day, and that is all He asks of us.

Waiting on the Lord is not watching the clock tick by until blessings flow passively out of a heavenly dispenser. Waiting on the Lord, at least in the context of a personal promised land, will often involve studying, planning, and working to make your vision a reality. At times, it may

---

[135] See 2 Nephi 30:6 (3-8); see also 1 Nephi 13:30-42, 15:13-16
[136] See 1 Nephi 9:6 (2-6)
[137] See Doctrine and Covenants 3:19 (1-3, 16-20)

seem that removing one obstacle from your path forward will allow room for two to grow back in its place. Recognizing that your agency is never limited, it may be tempting to push your way forward by brute force. However, the Lord's blessings are best received when they are enabled by Him and in complete harmony with His will. When you have done your best, you need to patiently wait for the Lord to open the right doors at the right time. Every so often, a figurative Red Sea will part, and you will step with gratitude to the other side.

Though the scale of your trials may not match those of any scriptural example, recognizing parallels in the essence of your experiences will be a source of strength, comfort, and reassurance. As you continually turn to the Lord, your faith will be strengthened. With Nephi, you feel to proclaim:

> *O Lord, I have trusted in thee, and I will trust in thee forever…Yea, I know that God will give liberally to him that asketh. Yea, my God will give me, if I ask not amiss; therefore I will lift up my voice unto thee; yea, I will cry unto thee, my God, the rock of my righteousness. Behold, my voice shall forever ascend up unto thee, my rock and mine everlasting God. Amen.*[138]

When you have reached your personal promised land, whatever form that may be, you should have no expectation that your days of trial are behind you. Rather, you can be confident that the challenges you faced in getting there were only preparatory for your next stage of life, and that you will one day look back with fondness on your former naivete. As grateful as you may be to inherit a "promised land," you will know that is not the true blessing of your experience—it will only be the vehicle. God will use your righteous desires to lead you on a journey where you can learn to trust, serve, worship, and know Him better. That

---

[138] 2 Nephi 4:34-35

is the eternally significant blessing He needs you to obtain. That is the miracle of a personal promised land.

The Plan of Happiness

It was not easy to keep the records that we now know as the Book of Mormon. The physical process of making the records presented difficulties that are unknown to modern writers. Mormon (and likely everyone else) etched his words into thin metal plates that he had made with his own hands.[1] Jacob had to be very selective in what he wrote because it was such a tiring process to write anything on plates.[2] Though their recording mechanism is foreign to us, the mental and emotional toll of writing was as demanding then as many writers experience now. Moroni talked about how the writing process exposed his personal weakness, cast doubts on his talents, and elicited fears for how his words would be received by others.[3]

Such descriptions of the difficulties they faced begs the question of their motivations. What was so important that they would make such an effort for the benefit of people they would never know? Fortunately, we do not have to theorize their "why." Many of the writers answered that question explicitly. A study of their motivations reveals several themes, one of which is especially relevant to the current topic.

Nephi wrote, "The fulness of mine intent is that I may persuade men to come unto the God of Abraham, and the God of Isaac, and the God of Jacob, and be saved."[4] His brother Jacob wrote, "I speak unto you these things that ye may rejoice, and lift up your heads forever, because of the blessings which the Lord God shall bestow upon your children."[5]

---

[1] See 3 Nephi 5:11 (8-11)
[2] See Jacob 4:1-2
[3] See Ether 12:25 (23-29)
[4] 1 Nephi 6:4 (3-6)
[5] 2 Nephi 9:3 (1-4); see also Jacob 1:4 (2-8) and Jacob 4:4 (2-6)

Mormon was motivated by a desire that his brethren "may once again come to the knowledge of God, yea, the redemption of Christ; that they may once again be a delightsome people."[6]

They wrote because they wanted us to repent. They wanted us to come unto Christ. They wanted to teach the Plan of Happiness. They wanted us to be happy.

As the abridger of the record, Mormon was responsible to search 1,000 years' worth of records to find that which was of most "worth unto the children of men"[7]. He then recorded those things on golden plates, which were eventually delivered to Joseph Smith, who translated them into the Book of Mormon. Though we now read Mormon's record in paper books and on electronic devices, the message is still golden. The Book of Mormon is a golden testament of God's plan of salvation and exaltation.

THE HAPPINESS PREPARED FOR THE SAINTS

There are seven different titles used for "the plan" by the various writers of the Book of Mormon. The term used most often is "the plan of redemption," with seventeen instances. "The plan of salvation" shows up three times. "Plan of happiness" is used only twice, as is "plan of mercy." The terms "plan of deliverance" and "plan of restoration" are each used once. Additionally, there are three variations of "plan of God" that are each used one time. The "plan of redemption," then, is used more often than all the other titles combined. However, members of the Church of Jesus Christ Latter-Day Saints tend to prefer "plan of salvation" and "plan of happiness" to describe the grand plan that God has for His children, and "plan of redemption" is used more rarely. For

---

[6] Words of Mormon 1:8 (2-8); see also Mormon 3:20-22 and Mormon 5:14 (12-15)
[7] 2 Nephi 28:2; see also Helaman 3:13-16, and 3 Nephi 5:8-10

some, it may seem paradoxical that the Church's vernacular does not reflect its keystone scripture.[8]

Like a study of the names of Christ, there is valuable insight to be gained by understanding the nuances of each title given to the same thing. Each name highlights a different aspect of an idea far too grand, far too complex to be contained within a single mortal phrase. The frequency of use of any one name reflects the context in which it is used and the user's experience and bias.[9] Regardless of which title is used in a given context, a student of the gospel will recognize the depths of meaning that are associated with it, and the use of any one name will secondarily invoke all the ideas associated with any other relevant name.

In other words, we like to use "plan of happiness" in our modern speaking and writing because the pursuit of happiness is particularly important to us in the Latter Days. But when we read in the scriptures about redemption, mercy, salvation, deliverance, or restoration, we understand that those are equivalent names for God's plan of happiness and any one topic reminds us of all the others.

Though "the plan of happiness" is explicitly named only twice in the Book of Mormon, the concept of happiness is implicitly linked to teachings about God's Plan throughout the book. This sacred record is wrought with evidence that happiness is a vital part of God's Plan for His children.

---

[8] "History, 1838–1856, volume C-1 [2 November 1838–31 July 1842]," p. 1255, The Joseph Smith Papers, accessed November 17, 2022, https://www.josephsmithpapers.org/paper-summary/history-1838-1856-volume-c-1-2-november-1838-31-july-1842/427

[9] Most of the uses of the "plan of redemption" in the Book of Mormon are directly attributable Alma the Younger. He may have learned the term from reading the writings of Jacob (see Jacob 6:8). It is logical that this title would have been particularly meaningful to him, given his poignant experience with being redeemed (see Alma 36:15-21) and a lifetime of experience helping others to find the same gift.

The most succinct link between God's Plan and happiness anywhere in the scriptures comes to us courtesy of Lehi in his teachings to Jacob. "Adam fell that men might be; *and men are*, that they might have joy."[10] The Fall of Adam and Eve—that often underappreciated pillar of the Plan—was necessary so that we could all come into mortal existence. And the entire reason for our mortality, according to Lehi, is so that we can have joy. The age-old question as the purpose of life is given in seven concise words: "men are that that they might have joy."

That conclusion is at once beautifully simple and uncomfortably puzzling. Anyone with any level of consciousness knows that unadulterated joy is typically a fleeting experience, and day-to-day living is filled with many emotions that fall short of ecstasy. This paradox is why the pursuit of happiness is such a universally relevant topic of study.

The verse preceding its famous neighbor gives us an important clue to interpret the puzzle. "All things have been done in the wisdom of him who knoweth all things."[11] When we understand God's Plan through the lens of His wisdom—unattainable as that may seem—we understand how everything in the Plan points us to divine joy.

Jacob internalized these teachings from his father and gave added insight on the link between the Plan and happiness when he instructed his people.[12] Jacob pled for his family to come unto Christ. He taught about the straight and narrow path with its gate being kept by the Holy One of Israel. The gate keeper—Christ—will open the gate for anyone who knocks, but anyone who comes in pride (because of their wealth and own wisdom) will be despised and not allowed to enter. Those who are thus cast out will have the "things of the wise and the prudent"

---

[10] 2 Nephi 2:25 (17-29), emphasis added; The Atonement of Christ is the only way to counteract the effects of the Fall. There would be no hope in the post-fall world without Christ. Thus, it may be concluded "Christ is that men might have joy."

[11] 2 Nephi 2:24

[12] See 2 Nephi 6:1 (chapters 6-10)

(referring to the "happiness which is prepared for the saints") forever hidden from them.[13]

These teachings of Jacob underscore Lehi's teachings that God intends to share His divine happiness with anyone who earnestly seeks it. However, wanting it is not enough. Being wise is not enough. To have the gates of divine happiness opened to us, we need to be humble, wise (after the manner of God's wisdom) and prudent. In other words, we need to be saints.[14]

We need not wait for the gates of heaven to experience divine happiness. Our souls are eternally existent, and if we "are that [we] might have joy," it can be concluded that happiness is prepared for us at any given point in eternity. Consider these examples from the scriptures that make it clear that happiness is not confined to any one part of the Plan.

King Benjamin implored his people to "consider on the blessed and happy state of those that keep the commandments of God. For behold, they are blessed in all things, both temporal and spiritual." The happiness of commandment keepers is something that can be seen and emulated by others working their way along the path. Besides being blessed now, faithful commandment keepers are promised to be received into heaven and there experience never ending joy.[15]

Almost six decades after King Benjamin taught these things, Helaman experienced their truthfulness with his two thousand young warriors. Their first assignment in battle was to reinforce Antipus' forces, who had suffered tremendous casualties at the hands of the Lamanites. In grappling with this sorrow, the survivors knew that those who had been killed were martyrs for their God and country, and that

---

[13] 2 Nephi 9:41-43
[14] See Dale G. Renlund, "Latter-day Saints Keep on Trying", *Liahona*, May 2015, 56-59.
[15] Mosiah 2:41

they were happy in the kingdom of God. This faith brought consolation, perhaps even a bit of joy, to the survivors.[16]

Ancient prophets foresaw that the death of Christ would be accompanied by days of darkness and natural disasters around the world. This devastation was necessary as a sign to all the scattered parts of Israel that Christ had been slain. This universal divine message was a source of terror for many people. But those who were righteous heard the voice of God in the middle of all the chaos and it was a time of "great joy and salvation."[17]

We know that days of universal terror are yet to come in the world's history. The scriptures are full of prophesies concerning the last days of Earth as we know it, and the judgements of God that will occur during that time. It will be a time of terrible devastation and fear will be everywhere—almost. While "the heavens shall vanish away like smoke, and the earth shall wax old like a garment; and they that dwell therein shall die in like manner", the "redeemed of the Lord shall return, and come with singing unto Zion; and everlasting joy and holiness shall be upon their heads".[18] As in the days of the death of Christ, the righteous are promised joy even as the whole world literally crumbles around them.

Whether or not we live to see the Second Coming of Christ while mortal, we know that divine happiness is available to us as soon as we die. Alma taught about "paradise" as a state of happiness, rest, and peace that the righteous will receive between the time of death and resurrection.[19]

Mormon taught that those who are found guiltless at Judgement Day (or the post-resurrection phase of the Plan) will dwell in the presence of

---

[16] Alma 56:11 (9-11)
[17] 1 Nephi 19:11 (10-17); For a fulfillment of this prophesy, see 3 Nephi 8-10. See also Russell M. Nelson, "Hear Him", *Liahona*, May 2020, 88-92.
[18] 2 Nephi 8:6,11 (3-11)
[19] Alma 40:12 (11-12, 15, 21)

God in endless happiness and praise.[20] This is the definitive goal of God's plan of happiness, and all other experiences, sorrows, and joys we are meant to have before then are preparatory for that day.

How Great is the Plan!

Jarom is one of the lesser-known writers of the Book of Mormon. Not only did he make a small contribution to the text, but he was also more guarded than others in sharing his personal story and testimony. His writings focus on a high-level history of his people and are doctrinally light, so it is easy for readers to float over his book on their way from Enos to Mosiah. However, Jarom was intentional in his minimalistic writing approach. He said, "I shall not write the things of my prophesying, nor of my revelations. For what could I write more than my fathers have written? For have not they revealed the plan of salvation? I say unto you, Yea; and *this sufficeth me.*"[21] In Jarom's mind, his predecessors had adequately recorded the plan of salvation, so he had nothing else significant to contribute.

Jarom was the son of Enos, grandson of Jacob, great-grandson of Lehi, and great-nephew of Nephi. When studying the writings of these fathers of Jarom, it is easy to empathize with his position of not wanting to distract from what had already been said.

Though Enos wrote little more than his son Jarom, Enos was more candid in his approach. He recorded the story of how he received a remission of his sins[22], testified about faith in Christ and the power of covenants[23], and rejoiced in his coming resurrection and acceptance into God's kingdom.[24]

---

[20] Mormon 7:7 (5-8); see also Alma 28:12
[21] Jarom 1:2, emphasis added.
[22] See Enos 1:2-12
[23] See Enos 1:15-18
[24] See Enos 1:27

Jacob taught extensively about the "merciful plan of the great Creator."[25] 2 Nephi chapter 9 is an especially classic and doctrinally dense chapter about the redemption offered by the atonement of Christ. Jacob forcefully testified of the fallen nature of man, rejoiced in the reality of the resurrection, and glorified in the greatness of God.[26] With a strong doctrinal foundation, he passionately pled for his audience to "come unto the Lord, the Holy One" and to prepare for "that glorious day when justice shall be administered unto the righteous."[27]

Like 2 Nephi 9, the second chapter of the same book is a pillar in the Book of Mormon's testament of God's Plan. 2 Nephi 2 is the record of Lehi's final teachings to Jacob[28] and has some of the most quotable doctrinal statements found anywhere in the book.[29] Lehi made two notable, and closely related, contributions to our understanding of God's Plan. They are his explanation about the need for opposition and his testimony of happiness being a central aim of the atonement of Jesus Christ.

Punishment for sin and happiness in righteousness are eternal principles inseparably connected to the law of the Holy One. They are deliberately made opposites of each other so that the purposes of the Atonement of Christ can be achieved. Without this opposition, there would be no distinction between righteousness and wickedness, holiness (or happiness) and misery, good and bad, life and death, corruption and incorruption, or sense and insensibility. Without these distinctions, there would have been no purpose for the creation of the earth because there would have been no way to measure the faithfulness of God's

---

[25] 2 Nephi 9:6
[26] See 2 Nephi 9:13 (5-26)
[27] 2 Nephi 9:41, 46 (40-46)
[28] See 2 Nephi 2:1
[29] For example, "It must needs be, that there is an opposition in all things" (v.11), "God…created…things to act and things to be acted upon" (v. 14), "men are, that they might have joy" (v. 25), and "the devil…seeketh that all men might be miserable like unto himself" (v. 27).

children. Thus, the wisdom, power, mercy, and justice of God would have been destroyed.[30]

Similarly, rejecting the existence of divine law implies the nonexistence of sin, then of righteousness, then of happiness, then of punishment and misery. Without these, there is no evidence of divine design. Conversely, we know there is a God who intentionally created us because we experience happiness—and misery—as consequences of choices we make in mortality. We can likewise be assured of the existence of divine law because the vicissitudes we experience.[31]

As mortal beings and children of God, we live on earth to act and not to be acted upon. We must use our God-given gift of agency to accept the plan He has created for us. We prove our personal acceptance of that plan through daily choices between righteousness and wickedness. When we choose righteousness, we choose to repent, to change, and to become more godlike in our character.[32] However, our faithfulness cannot be proven without opposing enticements. For this reason, God has allowed "bad" things to happen on earth since the beginning of time.[33]

No mortal man or woman in the history of the world has been perfect in their use of agency to choose righteousness. The demands of divine law are simply too great to be appeased by a mortal effort. For this reason, our all-knowing and all-merciful Father in Heaven provided a Savior "to answer the ends of the law, unto all those who have a broken heart and a contrite spirit".[34] To avoid a predetermination of our use of agency, that infinite, atoning sacrifice was offered on behalf of every child of God who ever has and ever will live on the earth. As such, every mortal soul will be brought to stand before the bar of God and

---

[30] See 2 Nephi 2:10-12
[31] See 2 Nephi 2:13
[32] See Russell M. Nelson, "We Can Do Better and Be Better", *Liahona,* May 2019, 67-69.
[33] See 2 Nephi 2:14-16, 21-24
[34] 2 Nephi 2:7

there be judged according to His truth and holiness. Only those that have proven their belief in Christ by their faithful use of agency will experience the full benefit of His redemptive power.

One of the greatest statements on the need for missionary work was given when Lehi exclaimed, "How great the importance to make these things known unto the inhabitants of the earth!"[35]

Lehi acted on his enthusiasm to share the plan of redemption with the whole earth by starting with his own family. Undoubtedly, Nephi's rejoicing in the "great and eternal plan of deliverance from death" was heavily influenced by the tutoring he received from his parents.[36] Nephi's soul likewise delighted in "proving unto [his] people the truth of the coming of Christ." He gloried in the covenants of the Lord and in His grace, justice, power, and mercy. This fiery testimony motivated his writings, and particularly his extensive quotations of Isaiah. Nephi yearned for his posterity to rejoice as he had.[37]

From Lehi to Jarom, this family is a shining example of the power in God's Plan to unite generations and invoke faith, hope, and joy for all who understand and apply its teachings. How great is the Plan!

RESTORATION AND REDEMPTION

Alma the Younger is one of the most prominent figures in the Book of Mormon, both in terms of his influence on the history of the posterity of Lehi, as well as his rich doctrinal contributions to the sacred text. Valiant though he was, he was not immune to discouragement. At one such low point near the end of his ministry, he shifted his attention from ministering to others to ministering to his own family. He

---

[35] 2 Nephi 2:8 (3-10)
[36] Though we do not know as much about her, we can safely assume that Sariah also had a profound influence on Nephi's testimony and love for the Plan of Salvation. See 1 Nephi 1:1.
[37] See 2 Nephi 11:4-5 (4-8)

gathered his three sons to give each one personalized instruction related to their discipleship.[38]

First came Helaman, who was the oldest brother[39] and Alma's chosen successor as the keeper of the Nephite records and other sacred artifacts.[40] In 77 verses of text, Alma gave a detailed account of his own conversion and subsequent ministry, conferred possession of the sacred records, warned against works of darkness, and gave other sound words of comfort and counsel.[41]

Next came Shiblon, his middle son and faithful missionary companion.[42] In fifteen verses, Shiblon was reminded of his righteousness and received encouragement and counsel to remain faithful. It is easy to imagine Shiblon as an unassuming but highly relatable character. He did not have the notoriety of Helaman, but was still faithful, steady, and patient in doing the work of God.[43]

Then, it was Corianton's turn. Corianton was not like his older brothers. He was the renegade of the family. He had a reputation for being less diligent in keeping the commandments and was arrogant. Worst of all, he had slipped away from his missionary service to pursue a harlot.[44] It is possible that Alma saw shadows of his young, rebellious self in his youngest son.[45] Certainly Alma saw unholy behaviors that needed to be corrected, even if it would bring pain for his son.[46] Being informed by his past ministry experience, "Alma thought it was

---

[38] See Alma 35:15-16
[39] See Alma 31:7
[40] See Alma 37:1-2, 47
[41] See Alma 36-37
[42] See Alma 31:7
[43] See Alma 38
[44] See Alma 39:1-4
[45] See Mosiah 27:8
[46] See Alma 39:7

expedient that [he] should try the virtue of the word of God" [47] to help bring his son back into the fold of God.

If the Book of Mormon is a golden testament of God's Plan of Redemption, then Alma's 91 verses of counsel to Corianton are a vein of diamonds. Of the seven names for "the plan" used in the Book of Mormon, five of them are in these teachings to Corianton. Imagining the classic diagram of the plan of salvation, these teachings focus on the portion of the plan between the end of mortality through the final judgement.

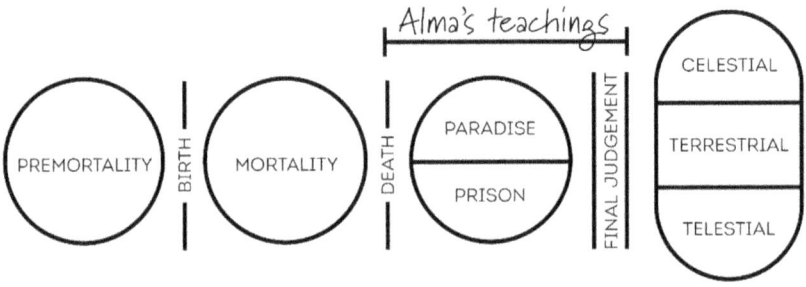

However, Alma was not primarily concerned with the structural elements of the plan. His discussion with Corianton instead focused on critical aspects of the Plan of Redemption that cannot be easily sketched on a chalkboard.

When Alma sat down with Corianton, he saw a son whom he loved and had immense potential for good but had made some poor decisions. Alma's fiery faith had been stoked from similarly gray embers over years of discipleship and consecrated ministering efforts. He had seen many people—including himself—learn to "sing the song of redeeming love" and experience a complete change of heart.[48] Now in the twilight of life, Alma yearned to see that transformation yet again, but this time in the intimate context of his own offspring.

---

[47] Alma 31:5
[48] See Alma 5:26

The record says that Alma chose his topic of discussion because he sensed that Corianton was concerned about the resurrection of the dead.[49] On the surface, resurrection seems like a far-out topic for someone who has willfully rebelled against his parents and God. The resurrection (at least as we tend to think about it) feels like a doctrinal topic better suited for a Sunday School class than for a parent on a couch at home pleading for his child to repent and accept the basic tenants of the gospel.

In discussing resurrection and the Plan of Salvation, neither Alma nor Corianton were concerned about diagraming the Plan of Salvation like missionaries do. Nor were they hypothesizing how the matter that had once composed the bodies for all who had ever lived would one day be restructured into billions of immortal beings, like Sunday School classes do. Their discussion was much more profound and applicable than either of those scenarios. The resurrection of the dead was simply a lens to discuss weightier matters of the Plan of Salvation. Specifically, Alma taught extensively about the eternal dance of justice and mercy and their role in bringing about God's purposes.[50] In short, these chapters are a record of Alma's teachings on how to use the atonement of Christ to find eternal happiness.

Two of the five names that Alma used for "the plan" are especially relevant to the discussion of justice and mercy. The Plan of Restoration highlights God's justice, while the Plan of Redemption highlights God's mercy. As alluded to previously, these two names showcase different facets of the same thing. When we study the Plan through these alternate lenses, we get a grander understanding of the majesty of God's design. We can understand the paradox of God's justice being merciful, and his mercy being just. We see how the Plan of Restoration (justice) can only take effect because of the Plan of Redemption (mercy), and vice versa. We see how both principles are centrally focused on bringing about the eternal happiness of all of God's children.

---

[49] See Alma 40:1

[50] For example passages, see Alma 42:22-26 and Alma 12:25

PLAN OF RESTORATION

Restoration, in a general sense, implies the idea of being made whole, or renewed to a former state. In the context of the Plan of Salvation, "restoration" highlights the justice of God, or the idea that everything must be made right. In introducing the term "Plan of Restoration," Alma taught Corianton (and us) that it is "requisite (with the justice of God) that *all things* be restored to their proper order."[51]

The restoration of "all things" will include our bodies and our spirits. Because of the resurrection of Christ, every part of every one of our bodies will one day be restored to itself. We know this doctrine as the universal resurrection. The concept of the restoration of our spirits may be more difficult to envision than it is to imagine hair growing back and joints aching no longer.[52] Nevertheless, we also know that our spirits will be restored to themselves according to the desires we develop during our mortal probation. If we develop good desires in our hearts and learn to repent, we are assured of a restoration to happiness, righteousness, and salvation. But if we fail in this task—if our desires are evil—we are assured of a restoration to misery, evil, and darkness. Either reward is made necessary by the demands of justice.[53]

This same concept is taught by others in the scriptures. Abinadi taught in Noah's court about the "resurrection of endless life [or]...endless damnation" that awaits each of us on the other side of God's judgement bar.[54] As a commentary on the deaths of tens of thousands of people during Alma's era, Mormon reminded us that we will each receive an eternal reward according to the spirit, good or bad, we have a tendency to obey.[55] He expounded on this teaching in his own record, when he taught that at the final judgement, "he that is filthy shall be filthy still; and he that is righteous shall be righteous still; he

---

[51] Alma 41:2, emphasis added.
[52] See Alma 40:23
[53] See Alma 41:2-8
[54] See Mosiah 16:10-11 (8-12)
[55] See Alma 3:26-27

that is happy shall be happy still; and he that is unhappy shall be unhappy still."[56] In other words, final judgement does not finally change attitudes. Justice requires that we earn our eternal reward as a reflection of the people we choose to become day by day.

Justice is not about God being vindictive. It is about rewarding souls in the best way possible. It is about allowing them as much eternal happiness as they are able and willing to enjoy.[57]

Eternal happiness cannot happen without justice because repentance cannot happen without an associated punishment. There must be a law to teach us God's manner of living, such as showing respect for mortal life by not committing murder. There needs to be a punishment attached to the law to motivate correct choices. If the law (and punishment) is not enforced, then we have no incentive to repent. These are the divine "demands of justice."[58]

RESTORATION FOR THE WICKED

Traditionally, any discussion about God's justice is centered on those who are wicked. Certainly, the volume balance of scriptural material is weighted in that direction. There are many examples of teachings warning of the negative consequences that justice will bring about for those who refuse to repent. Consider these examples that show how Plan of Restoration applies to the wicked:

- The waters of life have an open invitation, but no one is compelled to come. However, he who chooses not to come will have evil restored unto him in the last days.[59]

---

[56] Mormon 9:14 (11-14)
[57] See Mormon 9:2-5; Cleanliness and innocence before God is a requirement for eternal happiness. For the unrepentant, it is better (and a sign of God's mercy) to endure hell than to be filthy and miserable in God's presence.
[58] See Alma 42:16-22
[59] See Alma 42:27-28

- Those who walk by their own light will lie down in sorrow at journey's end.[60]
- Zion will mourn when she is punished for her iniquity.[61]
- The destruction prophesied to accompany the Second Coming of Christ will cause all-consuming sorrow.[62]
- The Lord hears the cries of those who suffer because of the sins of others. He will not stand for it. Abusers will receive their day of justice.[63]
- Unrepented transgressions will be brought "down with sorrow" upon the heads of the guilty. The Lord will only curse the land because of iniquity.[64]
- Mourning is promised for those who "doeth not works of righteousness." Other names for this group of people may include: shepherd-less sheep, workers of iniquity, those puffed up in vanity, hypocrites, or the fold of the devil. Those who meet these descriptions will receive their wages from the devil, who can reward nothing except death.[65]
- Those with "no part nor portion of the Spirit" will be cast "into weeping, and wailing, gnashing of teeth until resurrection.[66]
- Wicked people are often ignorant of the impending consequences for refusing to repent. If they understood what was waiting for them, they would repent.[67]

---

[60] See 2 Nephi 7:11
[61] See 2 Nephi 13:26, see also Lamentations 1:4-6 and Lamentations 2:8-11
[62] See 2 Nephi 23:8 (4-9); see also 2 Nephi 15:30
[63] See Jacob 2:31 (31-33)
[64] See Enos 1:10 (9-11); Note that Enos's experience with receiving this revelation about the justice of God strengthened his faith.
[65] See Alma 5:36 (33-42)
[66] See Alma 40:13-14
[67] See Helaman 9:21-22

- Those who refuse to repent will mourn. Having been a "favored people" in the past does not exempt anyone from divine law. The Lord chastens those whom he loves and stand in need of chastening.[68]

- Those living in the land of Bountiful prior to Christ's ministry learned a difficult lesson when the darkness and destructions foretold by prophets became lived experience. They suffered significant regret for refusing to repent.[69]

- Mormon mourned for the demise of those who had rejected Jesus. Their day of probation was past, and he knew that their slain bodies would one day be resurrected and stand before the judgement bar of God. At that point, their fate would be dependent on His justice and mercy. Mormon would have been more optimistic if they had repented before their death.[70]

- Fools delight in mocking the weaknesses of others. However, their day of judgement will eventually come, and they will mourn.[71]

In summary, those who refuse to repent will suffer because they have not accepted God's plan to appease the demands of justice. Since they have not been willing to receive this "more excellent way"[72] they will be left to their own abilities to satisfy the divine law.

Restoration for the Righteous

Though justice is typically associated with wickedness, the scriptures also teach how righteousness is rewarded through the demands of justice.

---

[68] See Helaman 15:2 (1-3)
[69] See 3 Nephi 8:23, 25 (19-25)
[70] See Mormon 6:18 (16- 22)
[71] See Ether 12:26
[72] 1 Corinthians 12:31

Jacob encouraged his brethren to "prepare your souls for that glorious day when *justice shall be administered unto the righteous.*" Those who have prepared for judgement by coming unto Christ will be spared from the fear and guilt that will consume the wicked.[73]

It often seems as though wicked people prosper and enjoy life, while disciples of Christ "walk mournfully" along the covenant path. It is easy to become fixated on this perceived disparity in mortality. However, we have a divine promise that the Lord is quietly recording a book of remembrance of those who fear the Lord, think upon His name, and gather often. That book of remembrance will be wide open on judgement day, and the faithful will receive a just recompence. They will be made the Lord's jewels and will be spared His wrath. Athletes will often quip, "the only score that matters is the one at the end of the game." So it is with our mortal probation. The judgement day will be the best time to clearly see the difference between rewards for wickedness and rewards for righteousness.[74]

Alma taught Corianton that at the time of death, all spirits are taken home to God. Those who are righteous inherit Paradise. Paradise is characterized as a state of happiness, peace and rest from all troubles, cares, and sorrows.[75] Mormon taught a similar doctrine in a message directed to latter-day Lamanites. He reminded them that they would need to "come to the knowledge of [their] fathers," referring to the doctrine of Christ. Because of the resurrection of Christ, every man and woman will be brought before Him to be judged. In that day, he who is found guiltless "hath it given unto him" to live in God's presence in a state of endless praise and happiness.[76]

In the Sermon on the Mount, Christ gave a listing of godly virtues that are each associated with a godly blessing. When we develop the

---

[73] 2 Nephi 9:46 (45-46), emphasis added.
[74] See 3 Nephi 24:14-18; see "This Vale of Sorrow" for added discussion on this scripture passage.
[75] See Alma 40:12 (11-12)
[76] See Mormon 7:7 (5-7)

virtue, the reward will be bestowed with divine integrity: those who mourn *shall* be comforted, the merciful *shall* obtain mercy, the pure in heart *shall* see God, and so forth.[77]

It is just for the righteous to be spared from punishment and given divine blessings because they have been obedient to the commandments and faithful to their covenants. They have chosen to become holy through consistent righteous decisions, so the demands of justice require that God be faithful in granting His promised rewards.

Plan of Redemption

In common usage, "redemption" and "restoration" have similar meanings. Redemption, too, carries the idea of being made new and free of defects. It also has a connotation of a monetary exchange, such as redemption of a coupon. Both nuances of "redemption" apply to the way Alma describes the Plan of Redemption to Corianton. When talking about God's Plan, redemption implies the power by which humanity is healed from the effects of the Fall of Adam and Eve. It also suggests payment of debts on our behalf to satisfy the demands of justice. While the "Plan of Restoration" is connected to our pursuit of God's purposes through justice, the "Plan of Redemption" is about achieving perfection through mercy.

When Adam and Eve ate the fruit of the tree of knowledge of good and evil in the Garden of Eden, they were physically and spiritually cut off from the presence of God. They were then mortal—susceptible to pain, illness, death, sin, and sorrow. These ill effects were the result of justice, and it became instantly necessary for humankind to be reclaimed from this condition of death for God's purposes to be completely realized.[78] Humanity had fallen into a hole and could not escape without divine aid. The only way to appease justice was through

---

[77] See 3 Nephi 12:2-12; see also Matthew 5:3-12
[78] See Alma 42:9 (6-9); Without the plan of redemption, our souls would be eternally miserable at the time of death. We would perish in a hardened state and be eternally lost to God. See also Alma 34:9 and Alma 42:11.

mercy, and the only way to bring about mercy was through an infinite atonement. Anything less than an atoning sacrifice offered by God himself would threaten the balance of justice and mercy and strip God of His power and authority. "God would cease to be God."[79]

While the atoning sacrifice of Christ is the heart of the Plan of Redemption, it is not the only element. The full power of the Plan of Redemption can only be realized when Christ's atoning power is balanced with our use of moral agency to exercise faith and repent.[80] The Great Plan of Salvation would have been foiled if there was no time and space for Adam, Eve, and their posterity to repent.[81] If God had simply plucked Adam and Eve out of their temporal death without allowing them an opportunity to exercise faith, the Plan of Happiness would have been destroyed.[82] Thus, we have been gifted this "time...to prepare to meet God."[83]

The Plan of Redemption was made for *you*[84] and "*now* is the time...of *your* salvation." The Plan of Redemption is *immediately* brought about to those who repent and soften their hearts.[85] We show reverence for God's plan when we apply our faith to repent and thus realize its full power. Only those who have "faith unto repentance" can access the power of the Plan of Redemption.[86]

The Plan of Redemption is God calling on men in the name of His Son, begging them to repent and soften their hearts. When we do that, He can have mercy on us through the power of the Redeemer and allow us to inherit His rest. This process was set forth by God at the beginning of time. After the Fall of Adam and Eve, He saw that it was necessary

---

[79] Alma 42:13 (12-15); see also Alma 34:8-10, 14-15
[80] See Alma 34:15-16
[81] See Alma 42:5 (4-7); see also Alma 12:26
[82] See Alma 42:8
[83] Alma 34:32(31-33)
[84] See Jacob 6:8 (5-11)
[85] See Alma 34:31
[86] See Alma 34:16 and Alma 42:12-13

that his mortal children should know concerning the things he had prepared for them. Thus, angels were sent to *converse* with mortals and cause them to behold God's glory. God's children learned the Plan of Redemption only "according to their faith, repentance and their holy works." With faith in the Plan of Redemption as a foundation, God's children were prepared to be taught His commandments. Part of the education on commandments included a warning for doing evil and thus being exposed to the deadly demands of justice. The intent of this warning was to create caution but not fear—a divine warning is not complete without a merciful plea to repent.[87]

Alma followed this pattern with Corianton. After all the glorious doctrine that he had taught, Alma's final words to his son had three notable elements: a final reminder of the name of God's plan as the "Plan of Mercy," an invitation to repent, and a call to share the great plan with others.[88]

As noted previously, one of the grandest statements on missionary work in the scriptures comes from Lehi after he taught the Plan of Redemption to Jacob. Lehi exclaimed, "how great the importance to make these things known!"[89] The link between redemption, repentance, and missionary work is well documented throughout scripture. Not only is there a doctrinal link, but several characters in the stories of the scriptures are sterling examples of this natural connection. Alma and the sons of Mosiah were driven to their epic missionary experiences by a desire to share the Plan of Redemption with a people who hated them.[90] Only a pure love borne of their own experiences with tasting redemption could have motivated the missionaries to do what they did.

---

[87] See Alma 12:28-34; see also Alma 34:17 (17-31)
[88] See Alma 42:31
[89] 2 Nephi 2:8 (3-9)
[90] See Alma 17:16 (13-17); see also Alma 18:39 (36-40) and Alma 22:13 (12-14)

Even after their grand journey was completed, Alma continued to yearn to preach repentance and redemption to the entire world.[91]

In the Restored Gospel of Jesus Christ, we know that the potential for eternal families is a key element of the Plan of Salvation. The integration of families into the Plan of Redemption is the ultimate goal of our missionary work. The underlying (though often unrecognized) reason missionaries commit to full-time service is not to preach the gospel to the whole earth, but to the parents of the whole earth. The divine pattern is for missionaries to share the gospel outside their families, so that parents (current or future) can share it within their families.[92] The significance of each conversion facilitated by missionaries is fully realized only when the Plan of Redemption becomes a generational affair.

---

[91] See Alma 29:1-2
[92] See Alma 39:16-19; see also Alma 24:14

Fruit to Make One Happy

One of the most beautiful and deeply symbolic lessons in the Book of Mormon comes in its opening chapters. What we know as "The Vision of the Tree of Life" is instructive in understanding many facets of the great Plan of Salvation and our journey towards the rich blessings our Father in Heaven has in store for us. The vision was first revealed to the prophet Lehi.[1] When he recounted it to his family, the magnificence of it—relayed by the power of the Holy Ghost—struck his son Nephi particularly hard. Nephi yearned to receive the same vision.

Full of desire and faith, Nephi took the time to quietly ponder what he had learned from his father. While in this meditation, he was carried away in the Spirit and received according to his desires.[2] The versions we have of Lehi's and Nephi's visions were both written by Nephi, so Nephi's account is understandably much more detailed and far ranging than his father's version. When taken together, these accounts are a treasure trove of symbolism to help us understand the Father's Plan of Happiness.

The allegory of the tree of life is not unique to the Book of Mormon. Similar symbology is found throughout many global religious and cultural traditions.[3] Within our own tradition, this allegory has notable influence in the way we connect with our theology. Latter-Day Saints

---

[1] See 1 Nephi 8:2 (2-34) for the full account of Lehi's vision as recorded by Nephi.

[2] See 1 Nephi 10:17, 11:1; See 1 Nephi 11-15 for Nephi's full account of the vision.

[3] For several examples, see C. Wilfred Griggs, "The Tree of Life in Ancient Cultures", *Ensign*, June 1988.

have depicted the tree of life and the vision in diverse visual art forms[4], music,[5] and even augmented reality.[6]

One of the reasons this symbology is so prevalent is God's universal love for His children and His desire to teach all people of all times the way back to Him. Similarly, we may assume each of God's children in every age and every locale has "felt the call of heaven at some point in his or her life. Deep within us is a longing to somehow reach past the veil and embrace Heavenly Parents we once knew and cherished."[7] The vision of the tree of life (with all its associated symbology) has a potent power in feeding our soul's hunger to reconnect with our intrinsic divinity.

As with all good parables, the Tree of Life is richly layered in meaning. Those who have "ears to hear"[8] will find diverse insights, connections, and applications of the symbology that will become as increasingly personal as they are poignant. Rather than attempting a comprehensive analysis of the vision, this writing will focus on those elements that are most relevant to our pursuit of happiness.

Lehi's account of the vision opens with him being led by an angel for several hours through a "dark and dreary wilderness." It is conceivable that this extended period of disorientation and blind trust in his divine guide caused fear, worry, doubt, and other negative feelings in Lehi. After he reached out to the Lord to beg for mercy, his field of vision

---

[4] For several examples, see Mark Staker, "Tree of Life: Lehi's Dream—A Shared Vision", *Ensign*, September 1996.
[5] See "Tree of Life", music by Mack Wilberg, text by David Warner, performed by the Mormon Tabernacle Choir and Orchestra at Temple Square. *Music and the Spoken Word,* Episode 4587, August 13, 2017.
[6] See Camille West, "New Tree of Life App Lets You Explore and Teach Lehi's Vision", *ChurchofJesusChrist.org Church News*, 8 January 2020. At the time of writing, this app is no longer publicly available.
[7] Dieter F. Uchtdorf, "Yearning for Home", *Liahona,* November 2017, 21-24.
[8] Mark 7:16

opened. First, he observed that he was in a large, open field. And then he saw the tree.[9]

Like many other trees, its "fruit was desirable to make one happy" but this was not an ordinary tree. This was the ultra-white and immensely beautiful Tree of Life.[10] With his stomach rumbling after his long journey, Lehi reached up, and plucked a fruit. The leaves rattled as the branch snapped back. After a quick but gentle rub on his robes, Lehi let his teeth sink through the skin and into the tender flesh. With pulp in his beard and juice running off the point of his elbow, his soul was filled with profound joy. Light and warmth radiated from the middle of his chest. It was the sweetest thing he had ever tasted. It was the "most precious", "most desirable", and "greatest of all the gifts of God". Instinctively, his gaze moved upward from the fruit as he searched for his family. Anything that required so many superlatives to describe demanded to be shared with those he loved the most.[11] In time, Lehi was able to share this experience with several—but not all—his loved ones.[12]

Our own experiences with eating fresh fruit (and other delicious foods) help us to relate to and expound upon the vivid descriptions of the fruit given by Lehi and Nephi. But we know this is not a story only about the joys of food. Everything that Lehi experienced and felt about the fruit was only a representation of the ultimate and most desirable gift—the eternally emanating, all-encompassing love of God.[13]

Other elements of the vision are important to consider as we strive to understand the significance of the fruit. Those who ate from the tree worked their way there along a path bordered by an iron rod, which is a depiction of the word of God.[14] All travelers on the path faced dangers

---

[9] See 1 Nephi 8:4-10
[10] Nephi made the distinction that the tree that Lehi saw was a *representation* of the tree of life. See 1 Nephi 15:22.
[11] See 1 Nephi 8:10-13, 11:8-9, 15:36
[12] See 1 Nephi 8:14-18
[13] See 1 Nephi 11:21-23
[14] See 1 Nephi 8:19-20, 11:25, 15:23-24

inherent to their environment (e.g., mists of darkness)[15] and opposition directly from other people (e.g., persecution from the great and spacious building).[16] These elements of the vision represent the pride of the world and Satan's attempts to lead us away from the path to God.[17] Those who overcame the opposition and held fast to the commandments of God had the right and the blessing of eating from the tree.[18] The destruction of hell was represented by a river flowing alongside the path,[19] while it seems as though a "fountain of living water" flowed from the base of the tree of life.[20]

One reason this vision is so powerful is that it links many kinds of symbolism used elsewhere in the scriptures. The tree of life. A path to God. Fruit. Water. The lessons learned from these other emblems used in other contexts can be blended in a symphonic grandeur to reach an even richer and deeper understanding of the "greatest of all the gifts of God."[21]

SISTER TREES

In all of scripture, there are two trees spoken of in specific enough terms as to be given titles: the tree of life and the tree of the knowledge of good and evil. Both trees were planted by the hand of God in the Garden of Eden among all the other trees that were "pleasant to the sight, and good for food".[22] Each was important to the experience that Adam and Eve had in the garden and are deeply emblematic for anyone

---

[15] See 1 Nephi 8:23-24
[16] See 1 Nephi 8:26-28
[17] See 1 Nephi 11:35-36, 15:24
[18] See 1 Nephi 8:30, Revelation 2:7, 22:14, and Proverbs 11:30
[19] See 1 Nephi 8:13,19, 15:26-29
[20] See 1 Nephi 11:25
[21] 1 Nephi 15:36; A lesser recognized but noteworthy benefit of the tree of life is that its leaves have the power of healing nations. See Revelation 22:2 (1-3).
[22] See Genesis 2:8-9, Moses 3:8-9, and Abraham 5:8-9

seeking to understand Heavenly Father's Plan of Happiness. Because each tree plays a distinct but related role in the fulfillment of God's plan, they may be thought of as "sister trees."

When Adam and Eve were placed in the Garden of Eden, they were given free rein to eat the fruit from every tree in the garden,[23] except for one—the tree of knowledge of good and evil.[24] They were warned to not eat, or even touch, this tree because the certain consequence would be death.[25] In due course, Eve and then Adam understood the death promised from eating this fruit was vital in fulfilling God's plan for His children. They each ate the fruit, had their eyes opened to their innocent state, began to grow in wisdom, and were driven from the paradisical presence of God.[26] Thus, it was by eating the fruit from the tree of knowledge of good and evil that Adam and Eve entered mortality. The "death" they experienced was simply their transition from one state of glory to the next one in their eternal progression. Eating that fruit put them one step closer to being like God.[27]

As Adam and Eve journeyed out of the garden, God had one critical goal: ensure they did not eat from the tree of life. To prevent that from happening, God placed "cherubim and a flaming sword" on the east side of the Garden to "keep the *way* of the tree of life".[28] Recalling that that the tree of life was in the middle of the Garden,[29] it is apparent that there was a path from the east side of the garden to the tree of life in the middle. The two symbols of divine protection (cherubim and a flaming sword) were placed to guard the path—the straight and narrow path—between the edge of paradise and God's ultimate gift.

---

[23] The tree of life was presumably included in the list of trees they could eat from, because they were already in the presence of God.
[24] See Genesis 2:16-17 and Moses 3:16-17
[25] See Genesis 3:1-3 and Moses 4:7-9
[26] See Genesis 3:5-13, 16-19, 23 and Moses 4:11-19, 22-25, 29
[27] See Genesis 3:5, 22 and Moses 4:11, 28
[28] See Genesis 3:23-24 and Moses 4:29-31, emphasis added
[29] See Genesis 2:9 and Moses 3:9; Both trees were near each other in the "midst of the garden".

The question then becomes why such a protection was necessary at that time. Why would God guard the path to eternal life, which we know He so desperately wants all His children to receive?

Eating the fruit from the tree of life brings immortality.[30] Like the fruit of its sister tree, it represents a transition from one state of glory to the next one in our eternal progression. The would-be consequences of eating the fruit too early were articulately explained by Alma to his son Corianton:

> *For behold, if Adam had put forth his hand immediately, and partaken of the tree of life, he would have lived forever, according to the word of God, having no space for repentance; yea, and also the word of God would have been void, and the great plan of salvation would have been frustrated. But behold, it was appointed unto man to die—therefore, as they were cut off from the tree of life they should be cut off from the face of the earth—and man became lost forever, yea, they became fallen man.[31]*

And that is why, again from Alma, "there was a time granted unto man to repent, yea, a probationary time, a time to repent and serve God."[32]

Lehi similarly taught Jacob significant lessons about the Plan of Salvation using the context of the sister trees. Lehi used these trees and their fruit as an example of the need for an "opposition in all things" for God's plan to be fulfilled. The virtues of righteousness, holiness, and goodness would be unknowable without their opposites of wickedness, misery[33], and badness.[34] The two trees in the Garden of Eden were

---

[30] See Genesis 3:22 and Moses 4:28
[31] Alma 42:5-6
[32] Alma 42:4
[33] Misery being the opposite of holiness implies that holiness is a synonym of happiness.

placed near each other to provide an opposition for Adam and Eve to face: the tree of knowledge of good and evil with its relatively bitter forbidden fruit[35] and the tree of life with its unspeakably sweet fruit. The latter was made more desirable by its contrast to the former. It was this disparity that gave man the ability to choose and the enticement to choose righteousness.[36]

Taking the teachings of these two prophet-fathers together, we see that God protecting the tree of life—ensuring Adam and Eve experienced mortality—was an act of mercy. The path back to eternal life—not just living forever (i.e., immortality) but having all the blessings of God— must go through mortality. By divine design, we need to experience heartache, pain, and sorrow to stand as a contrast to the peace, comfort, and happiness that our loving Father in Heaven wants so desperately to share with us.[37]

If Adam and Eve had eaten from the tree of life too early, God's grand plan of happiness would have been frustrated because they would have been locked eternally in a miserable condition, having no "preparatory state".[38] The purpose for our life on earth is to prepare to enter God's presence, symbolized by eating the fruit of the tree of life. We prepare for that glorious event by choosing to repent.

Keep in mind the image of the path to the tree of life in the middle of the Garden of Eden as you consider these teachings from the prophet Nephi:

---

[34] See 2 Nephi 2:11 (10-13)

[35] Compare 2 Nephi 2:15 and Genesis 3:6; Though Adam and Eve perceived this fruit to be beautiful and "good for food" it was still bitter when compared to the tree of life fruit. There is a lesson here about the disparity between what mortals consider to be good and wholesome compared to God's standards.

[36] See 2 Nephi 2: 15 (11, 15-16)

[37] The path to the tree in Lehi's dream was not easy for anybody, as described in 1 Nephi 8:21-24, 30

[38] See Alma 12: 26 (21, 23, 26)

For the gate by which ye should enter is repentance and baptism by water; and then cometh a remission of your sins by fire and by the Holy Ghost[39].

And then are ye in this strait and narrow path which leads to eternal life; yea, ye have entered in by the gate; ye have done according to the commandments of the Father and the Son; and ye have received the Holy Ghost, which witnesses of the Father and the Son, unto the fulfilling of the promise which he hath made, that if ye entered in by the way ye should receive.

And now, my beloved brethren, after ye have gotten into this strait and narrow path, I would ask if all is done? Behold, I say unto you, Nay; for ye have not come thus far save it were by the word of Christ with unshaken faith in him, relying wholly upon the merits of him who is mighty to save.

Wherefore, ye must press forward with a steadfastness in Christ, having a perfect brightness of hope, and a love of God and of all men. Wherefore, if ye shall press forward, feasting upon the word of Christ, and endure to the end, behold, thus saith the Father: Ye shall have eternal life.[40]

Let us each, then, choose to repent as we make our individual journeys towards the tree of life. Eating that fruit symbolizes the ultimate happiness, even God's happiness, as we progress to our next state of eternal glory. The choice to repent is central to the purpose of our divinely designed mortal experience. Not only does it lead us to

---

[39] There is an interesting parallel between receiving a remission of sins "by fire and by the Holy Ghost" at the commencement of the path, and the symbol of "cherubim and a flaming sword" protecting the way of the path.
[40] 2 Nephi 31:17-20

eternal happiness, but it helps us find happiness along the way. As explained by President Russell M. Nelson:

> "When we choose to repent, we choose to change! We allow the Savior to transform us into the best version of ourselves. We choose to grow spiritually and receive joy—the joy of redemption in Him. When we choose to repent, we choose to become more like Jesus Christ!"[41]

FRUIT AND HARVESTING

The goal of Lehi and anyone else progressing towards the tree of life is to eat the fruit, or in other words, to harvest. The symbol of harvesting is found throughout the scriptures, often associated with the symbol of fruit. Studying the use of these symbols elsewhere in the scriptures brings a rich depth of understanding to the fruit of the tree of life.

Associated with a mission call in the early days of the Restored Church, the Lord counseled, "He that is faithful, the same shall be kept and blessed with much fruit."[42] The Apostle Paul described how the "word of the truth of the gospel" brought "forth fruit" for the saints in Colosse as soon as they heard the Word and "knew the grace of God in truth". The fruit Paul referred to was faith in Christ, love for fellowman, and a hope "laid up" in heaven.[43]

In the Sermon on the Mount and its sister sermon to the Nephites, the Savior taught about discernment using the symbol of fruit. A gardener judges the identity and the value of a tree by the fruit that it produces. Based on this judgment, the gardener decides whether to cultivate or burn the tree. Likewise, we can make judgments of

---

[41] Russell M. Nelson, "We Can Do Better and Be Better", *Liahona,* May 2019, 67-69.
[42] Doctrine and Covenants 52:34
[43] See Colossians 1:3-6

prophets—reflected in our choices to follow their teachings—based upon the fruit they produce.[44] Neither trees nor mortals can forever hide their value, whether good or bad, because of the fruit they produce.

The Savior used similar themes in the Parable of the Sower, as recorded in Matthew 13. The master teacher described seeds that were sown in four different conditions, each with a fate that reflected their environment. Seeds that were scattered on the hardpacked wayside were quickly devoured by birds and never experienced any growth.[45] When the soil was shallow and rocky, the seeds sprouted and were then scorched by the sun because they had no root system.[46] Seeds sown among thorns were able to grow but were choked out by the weeds and never produced fruit.[47] It was only when seeds were sown in good ground that the gardener was able to realize a harvest of fruit.[48]

Of course, the Savior was doing more than educating his disciples in horticulture. He was teaching eternal truths about the ways humanity responds to the invitation to "receive the Word," or in other words, to receive Christ.[49] Each of the soil environments described by the Savior corresponds to a condition of the human heart. The wayside represents those who hear the gospel but whose hearts are stolen by Satan before they are able to understand it.[50] Stony ground symbolizes those who initially receive the Word with gladness but are quickly offended when tribulation or persecution comes.[51] Those who receive the Word but are then distracted by the cares, riches, and pleasures of mortal life are like

---

[44] See Matthew 7:15-20 and 3 Nephi 14:15-20; see also Matthew 12:33
[45] See Matthew 13:4
[46] See Matthew 13:5-6
[47] See Matthew 13:7
[48] See Matthew 13:8
[49] The "word" referenced in Christ's interpretation of the parable directly refers to the gospel of Christ, but by extension it could apply to the "Word," meaning Christ himself. See John 1:1-3, 12-14
[50] See Matthew 13:19 and Luke 8:12; see also Doctrine and Covenants 84:49-53
[51] See Matthew 13:20-21 and Luke 8:13

the ground suffocated with fruitless weeds before their value as fruiting plants is realized.[52] And finally, the good ground represents those with good and honest hearts who hear, understand and patiently endure the Word and then bring forth fruit.[53]

Alma's classic teachings on faith are based on the symbols of cultivating and harvesting fruit. To a people who were poor materially as well as poor in heart,[54] Alma taught the process of cultivating and harvesting fruit "which is most precious, which is sweet above all that is sweet, and which is white above all that is white, yea, and pure above all that is pure". To these people who were hungry and thirsty due to their poverty, Alma promised a "feast…until ye are filled, that ye hunger not, neither shall ye thirst."[55]

Alma's description of the fruit of faith is strikingly similar to Lehi's description of the fruit of the tree of life[56], and not by accident. They are the same fruit.[57] With that connection established, a disciple of Christ can take the process Alma (or any other inspired teacher) provides for nurturing faith and apply it to growing greater happiness.

As in the Parable of the Sower, Alma begins his allegory by comparing the word[58] to a seed. From there, Alma expounds on the "good ground" heart condition from the Parable of the Sower. He encourages his audience to plant the seed in their hearts and avoid the natural-man tendency to resist the spirit of the Lord and reject the gospel through unbelief.[59] Alma then invokes the same imagery as the Savior in the Sermon on the Mount by encouraging the seeker of faith

---

[52] See Matthew 13:22 and Luke 8:14
[53] See Matthew 13:23 and Luke 8:15
[54] See Alma 32:2-8
[55] Alma 32:42
[56] See 1 Nephi 8:11
[57] See Alma 32:40
[58] As noted previously, the "word" could refer alternatively to the gospel of Christ or Christ himself.
[59] See Alma 32:28; see also Mosiah 3:19

(or happiness) to make continual judgements of the seed's value based on the way it develops and the fruit it produces. The growth of the seed can be recognized by "swelling motions" in one's breast, an enlarged soul, enlightened understanding, and an expanded mind. It is through this process of patience, nurturing, and continual evaluation that faith and happiness grow.[60]

Though bad seeds need to be cast away, that judgement cannot be made until they are given sufficient opportunity to prove themselves. If the honest seeker of faith fails in his obligation to diligence, patience, and long-suffering, he cannot blame the nature of the seed or the undesirability of the fruit for the failed harvest. He can only point to his own barren ground.[61]

But if the honest seeker of faith succeeds in his obligations to the process, he is promised "a tree springing up unto everlasting life" and all the other blessings attendant to it.[62] He is promised a feast at the base of the tree of life.

WATER

Alongside the tree of life, another important symbol in Lehi's and Nephi's vision is water. This symbology is a distinct line of thought from the symbols of trees and fruit discussed previously. However, both roads end up in the same place. Because of that, understanding the way water is used in the vision enhances our understanding of the symbols of fruit and trees.

We know that a river ran near the tree of life.[63] The headwaters of this river were in the large field (which represents the world) near the trailhead of the straight and narrow path. The path, iron rod, and river

---

[60] See Alma 32:28-34
[61] See Alma 32:38-40
[62] See Alma 32:37, 41-43
[63] See 1 Nephi 8:13

all roughly paralleled each other, moving towards the tree of life.[64] The great and spacious building, filled with people mocking the saints on the path, was on the opposite side of the river gorge from the path, rod, and tree.[65] Lehi observed that some who had started the journey towards the tree of life became disoriented and wandered off the path, eventually falling into the river and drowning.[66]

When Nephi recorded his experience with receiving the vision, he became fixated on how dirty the water was in the river. He told his brothers, "The water...*was* filthiness."[67] In other words, it was the very embodiment of uncleanliness. Nephi was instructed by his angelic tour guide that the river, in its extreme filth, was a representation of hell.[68] This hell physically separated the wicked from the saints moving towards and eating from the tree of life.[69]

This symbolic description of a river is supported by river behavior in the natural world. Rivers tend to be cleanest at their headwaters. The longer they are, the more erosive potential they have. The world around them—the soil—literally becomes a part of the water as the banks are eroded away. If the geography in the vision started as a flat plain, the river gorge would have also become increasingly deep as it eroded its way towards the tree of life. The elevation contrast between the river and the path would have started out small but grown bigger closer to the tree.

The role of water in this vision becomes more complex by an observation of Nephi. In his recounting of the vision, Nephi made the tree of life and "fountain of living waters" directly synonymous with each other. The iron rod (the word of God) leads to the "fountain of

---

[64] See 1 Nephi 8:14, 19-20
[65] See 1 Nephi 8:26-27, 15:28
[66] See 1 Nephi 8:32
[67] 1 Nephi 15:26-27, emphasis added.
[68] See 1 Nephi 12:16
[69] See 1 Nephi 15:28-30, 36

living waters [*and*] the tree of life" (the love of God).[70] If this equivalence of symbols is to be taken literally, one might imagine a spring of pure, crisp water bubbling up and flowing outward from the base of the tree of life.

Returning to the creation story, the river flowing out of Eden is consistently mentioned alongside the two sister trees. This river first watered the garden and then ran to the whole earth.[71] While the scriptural account is lacking in detail, when coupled with Nephi's imagery, it is conceivable that the headwaters of Eden's river were at the tree of life in "the midst of the garden".[72]

There are at least two important lessons to be derived from the synthesis of all this water-related symbolism.

The first is the relationship between Christ and Satan. Both the love of God and the temptations of Satan are represented by water, the one pure and life-giving and the other filthy and dangerous. Thus, it may be deduced that Satan is a corrupted imitation of Christ. The doctrines of Satan often have the same general form as the doctrines of Christ and may even seem to run in the same general direction as the word of God. The subtleties of Satan can easily go undetected without the careful application of discernment.[73]

---

[70] See 1 Nephi 11:25

[71] See Genesis 2:10 (10-14), Moses 3:10 (10-14) and Abraham 5:10

[72] See Genesis 2:9, Moses 3:9 and Abraham 5:9

[73] The story of Alma and Amulek contending with the Anti-Christ Zeezrom is a good example of the subtle nature of Satan's corrupt doctrines. In a back-and-forth exchange with Amulek (a new convert and missionary, see Alma 10:5-11) Zeezrom established a true doctrine (the Son of God would come to the earth) and then twisted a follow-up truth (Christ will not save people in their sins) into an unpalatable doctrine (God will not save His people) by subtly cutting the true statement short. The intent of this manipulation was to cast Amulek as an enemy to the people by making it appear that he was preaching the doctrine of a cruel God and threatening their system of government (by which Zeezrom was employed). Zeezrom's

Despite the superficial similarities, they are comprehensively different in their nature and motivations. Christ came to earth to liberate us all from the effects of the Fall, giving us the ability to act for ourselves and to live forever. Satan, however, seeks to captivate us and lead us to death that he might have company in his eternal misery. Little wonder that Lehi urged his sons, "I would that ye should look to the great Mediator, and hearken unto his great commandments; and be faithful unto his words, and choose eternal life, according to the will of his Holy Spirit."[74]

The second lesson relies on the equivalency of the tree of life and the fountain of living water. To deepen our understanding of eating from the tree, we can apply all that we know about drinking from the fountain. Drinking from the fountain is all about coming unto Christ.

The symbolic connection between Christ and the living water is taught throughout scripture. The most notable teachings on the subject come from Jesus himself as he taught the Samaritan woman at Jacob's well. The Savior promised that anyone who accepts him will discover a "well of water springing up into everlasting life."[75] On a later occasion, he promised to anyone who believes in him, "out of his belly shall flow rivers of living water."[76]

In latter-day revelation, commandment keepers are jointly promised they will understand the mysteries of the kingdom and receive an internal "well of living water, springing up unto everlasting life".[77]

---

misrepresentation of Amulek's teaching was a minor change in wording that reflected a notable change in meaning and conclusion. Thankfully, the two missionaries had the Spirit of the Lord to discern Zeezrom's intentions and tactics and were able to counteract them with true doctrine. See Alma 11:34-37 (10:13-32, 11:21-40, 12:1-7). See also Genesis 3:1-5, Matthew 26:1-5 and Doctrine and Covenants 123:12.

[74] 2 Nephi 2:28 (26-28)
[75] See John 4: 10, 14 (5-26)
[76] See John 7:37-38
[77] Doctrine and Covenants 63:23

Mighty assurances are promised to those who, as the Apostle John foresaw in the last days, will come "out of great tribulation, and have washed their robes, and made them white in the blood of the Lamb". They will serve God day and night in his temple with Him in their midst. They will neither hunger nor thirst and will be protected from the elements. God himself will wipe the tears from their eyes as Christ feeds them and leads them to "living fountains of water."[78]

The power of living water is not limited to individuals. The earth itself will be renewed by the healing power of living water in the day of restoration. In that day, pools of living water will spring up in barren deserts, turning the parched ground into oases. Whether this is meant to have a figurative or literal interpretation (or both), we get the sense that "ransomed of the Lord" will gloriously return to Zion to find rest, rejuvenation, and joy. That transformation is enabled by the healing power of living water.[79]

The invitation to come unto Christ is not passively open to anyone who stumbles into His doctrines, commandments, and grace. Isaiah pleads,

> "[Oh!][80] every one that thirsteth, come ye to the waters, and he that hath no money; come ye, buy, and eat; yea, come, buy wine and milk without money and without price."[81]

---

[78] See Revelation 7:14-17 (9-17)

[79] See Isaiah 35:6-7 (1-10) and Doctrine and Covenants 133:29 (24-35)

[80] The original Hebrew word translated here as "ho" could alternatively be given as "Oh!". It implies an expression of woe, sorrow, grief, pity, or concern. Refer to "H1945", *Strong's Exhaustive Concordance of the Bible*, James Strong, 1896. and "Alas", *American Dictionary of the English Language*. Noah Webster, 14 April 1828.

[81] Isaiah 55:1

The prophets and the Savior not only invite us to come, they *beg* for us to come and drink from "the water of life freely".[82]

The continued writings of Isaiah beautifully instruct us how to come unto Christ describe the divine promises in store for those who come to drink. Let these sacred words of eternal life sink deep into your heart[83] as you contemplate your personal journey to greater faith and happiness:

> *Wherefore do ye spend money for that which is not bread? and your labour for that which satisfieth not? hearken diligently unto me, and eat ye that which is good, and let your soul delight itself in fatness.*
>
> *Incline your ear, and come unto me: hear, and your soul shall live; and I will make an everlasting covenant with you…*
>
> *Seek ye the Lord while he may be found, call ye upon him while he is near:*
>
> *Let the wicked forsake his way, and the unrighteous man his thoughts: and let him return unto the Lord, and he will have mercy upon him; and to our God, for he will abundantly pardon.*
>
> *For my thoughts are not your thoughts, neither are your ways my ways, saith the Lord.*
>
> *For as the heavens are higher than the earth, so are my ways higher than your ways, and my thoughts than your thoughts.*

---

[82] See Revelation 21:5-6 and Doctrine and Covenants 10:66
[83] See Enos 1:3

For as the rain cometh down, and the snow from heaven, and returneth not thither, but watereth the earth, and maketh it bring forth and bud, that it may give seed to the sower, and bread to the eater:

So shall my word be that goeth forth out of my mouth: it shall not return unto me void, but it shall accomplish that which I please, and it shall prosper in the thing whereto I sent it.

For ye shall go out with joy, and be led forth with peace: the mountains and the hills shall break forth before you into singing, and all the trees of the field shall clap their hands.

Instead of the thorn shall come up the fir tree, and instead of the brier shall come up the myrtle tree: and it shall be to the Lord for a name, for an everlasting sign that shall not be cut off."[84]

---

[84] Isaiah 55:2-13; see also 2 Nephi 9:50-53 and 2 Nephi 32:3

Postface

I cannot over-emphasize how much this book is a personal study project that grew much larger than I could have expected. I started my study on this topic not because I thought the world needed to hear from me, but because I needed to have a greater understanding of happiness for my own benefit. I had faith that the answers to life's most profound questions are uniquely found in the Restored Gospel of Jesus Christ, so it was important for me to keep that singular focus and experiment upon the word.[1] As my understanding grew, so did my desires to share my renewed faith. It was too good to *not* share. It was a journey of self-discovery of desires, abilities, and faith. The side benefit is that I get to share what I have learned with others.

I have two fears in putting this book out for others to read. I touched on my first fear in the preface. It is that the reader will discredit what I have written because I, as the author, do not understand the reader's life experience. There is probably a lot of truth in that assessment. I am a young, middle-class white man with a stable (if crazy) nuclear family. The Restored Gospel of Jesus Christ has been part of my cultural identity for generations in every direction. I have not battled serious illness, faith crisis, or financial ruin. I have not yet suffered the death of a parent, spouse, or child.

Given my life experience, I can see how it could look presumptuous for me to give gospel-based happiness advice to most anyone else. I have rolled my eyes at more than one young single adult who doled out off-

---

[1] See Alma 32:27 (26-28)

base parenting advice in a Sunday School class. I would cringe to know I was similarly seen by anyone else as one who speaks without the knowledge and wisdom[2] that can only come through lived experience. My life has not been free of difficulty, to be sure, but I know very few people that I would want to trade places with.

My intent as an author is not to answer questions, but to point the reader in a direction where answers may be found. This is why I have fixated on grounding everything I have written very closely to the scriptures and words of living prophets. I take comfort in knowing that I do not have to completely understand the world view of every reader. I do not have the emotional capacity to do that—but I know someone who does. It is Jesus. If you have experienced nothing else by reading this book, my sincere prayer is that you have experienced the love of your Savior. I hope you have felt at least a twinge of desire to exercise more faith in Him, and that you will let the desire work within you to grow in faith and knowledge of His infinite redeeming, enabling power.

My second fear is related to the first. It is that someone will suppose that I see myself as an expert on happiness, gospel study or devoted discipleship. It is true that I have had many profound experiences with the Holy Ghost in writing this. My faith and understanding are more mature than when I started. However, I will not guarantee that my writing is without fault or short-sightedness. I am still pressing my way towards the tree of life along with every other disciple of Christ. This book is a snapshot in time, and I expect my tree of faith to continue to grow limbs, branches, and fruit. As with my first fear, the self-prescribed antidote for my second fear is a plea for you to not take my word as being authoritative. Please do your own study, pondering and Spirit-led conclusion forming.

After I had finished a draft manuscript of this book, I gave a copy to my wife to review and give feedback. During this period, I had a particularly frustrating week at work. As I vented to her one day, she reminded me that she had recently been reading a book that talked

---

[2] See Job 34:35

about the importance of accepting sorrows as an inevitable part of life and finding joy despite our circumstances. Feeling trapped in a corner, I asked if she had found it on the tabloid rack at the grocery store. I am still learning to apply everything I have talked about in these pages.

I am open to the idea that my ability to ponder the scriptures and write about them is a gift that not everyone shares in the same way. If we understand the gifts of the Spirit, we know that by divine design, everyone has a different toolbox to approach the challenges of life. When we all do our best with the gifts we are given, the whole body of Christ is edified. This book is my offering on the altar. I put my best effort into this project and want to share it with others in the hope that they will be likewise inspired to greater faithfulness. When you are moved to greater faithfulness (because of this book or anything else), you will manifest it in your unique way. Your circle of influence will then be blessed by your contributions, and the divine pattern will then continue.

Another Invitation

In the preface, I invited you to prepare a "Plan of Happiness Compliance Document" as a personal guide for applying God's Plan of Happiness to your life. If that invitation did not resonate with you, I have another one for your consideration.

If I think about my experience as a literal source of light, then I attribute its brightness to two power sources. The first, and most important, source of power is that I have whole-heartedly let the Spirit be my guide in studying, pondering, and writing. I have learned to trust in the Lord like never before. The second power source is that this has been a creative project. I have a firm testimony that each of us has both the desire and ability to create beautiful things. Creative potential is in our divine DNA because we were created by heavenly parents who unfathomably created the entire universe and everything that it contains.³

My invitation to you now is to follow this pattern in your own way. Let the Spirit be your guide as ponder the gospel topics that you need to understand better. When you have a topic, find a way to not only study it, but create something tangible as a product of your study. Write a family home evening lesson or pretend General Conference talk. (Bless your heart if you decide to write a book.) Compose a poem or a song. Program your own database, app, or website. Illustrate the scriptures or design shareables for social media. You could even find an unconventional way to incorporate gospel study into your exercise routine, like creating a scripturally based yoga flow. The possibilities are truly endless. Your only limitation will be self-imposed thoughts like, "But I am not good at_____", "I am not _____", or "That would be weird." You are in complete charge of who you share your creative project with, so you do not need to worry whether it is "good enough." All you need to do is pick a topic of interest, allow a little space for your imagination to grow, and then roll up your sleeves and get to work. Based on my own experience, I predict that you will be surprised at what the Lord can do through you—if you allow Him the opportunity.

When you express your faith through creativity, two wonderful things happen. First, you will find your heart being drawn closer to God and your own faith growing in remarkable ways. This happens because you cannot be a passive consumer when you are creating something new. It takes a committed, coordinated effort of mind and soul to start with disorder and organize the subject into something meaningful. As alluded to previously, you become more like God because creation is a Godly work. Secondly, as Lehi learned, your taste of God's love will lead to an intuitive desire to share the experience. When that desire strikes, you will be ready with a tangible, meaningful gift to help others to strengthen their faith.

---

³ See Dieter F. Uchtdorf, "Happiness, your Heritage", *Liahona*, November 2008, 117-120.

My Transformative Experience

In the preface, I mentioned that this study project (starting with my spreadsheets) has been a transformative experience. That transformation comes with at least three different faces, which are reflected in the three purposes for this book that I outlined in the preface: experiencing divine happiness, the power of God's word, and coming unto Christ. I call these faces because they all describe the same process but from different viewpoints and cannot be completely compartmentalized from each other.

Divine Happiness

The first face of my transformation is my understanding of and experiences with divine happiness. I wish that I could report that completing an extensive study about happiness has erased life's troubles. It has not. In some ways, life is more complicated now than when I started this project. I do not expect that will change this side of death. The thought of freely given perpetual blue skies and green grass is still temptingly appealing, but I know that God has something better in store.

Rather than erasing troubles, I have been given a better framework to interpret every experience. This new framework has provided several tangible benefits. I have found myself becoming more patient in the twists, turns and bumps that are inevitable in mortality. I have found myself becoming more empathetic to the trials that other people face. I am a better parent because I am more able to help my children understand the value of their sad times. Similarly, I have been better (but not perfect) at raising my vision beyond hair-raising tantrums and seeing the people they are becoming.

Even though life is still hard, I have felt a depth of divine happiness that I have not ever experienced before. Some of that happiness is inherent to the process of studying and writing, by which I have experienced the joy of discovery, the joy of creating, and the joy of sharing. On a deeper level, I have connected with the joy that Ammon experienced when he exclaimed, "Blessed be the name of our God; let us sing to his praise, yea, let us give thanks to his holy name, for he doth work righteousness forever."[4] I have seen the majesty of God's plan laid out in the scriptures, and I have seen it working in my own life and in the lives of others. My vision has been raised to a higher plane. Seeing the world more from God's point of view allows more opportunities to experience God's joy.

Scripture Study

The second face of my transformation has been around the way I approach my scripture study. My relationship with God's holy word has been forever changed. Scripture study has moved from being a good habit "because that is what you are supposed to do" to a genuine hobby that I am eager to start and reluctant to finish.[5] Even when I am not actively studying, I will often find my thoughts drifting back to the things I have been studying recently. I hope that does not come across as being conceitedly pious, but it is the truth. I am keenly aware of all the other parts of my discipleship that still need help, but if gospel living were reduced to a checklist of righteous activities (which it is not) I could comfortably mark the box next to personal scripture study.

The scriptures have never been more alive for me because of the many profound experiences I have had with seeing direct applications to my life. I have worried about my writing just as Mormon did.[6] I have glorified the Lord with Ammon.[7] I have eaten the fruit with Lehi.[8] Along the way, I have had many similar experiences with the scriptures which I have not written about here, either because they are not directly relevant to the topic or are too sacred to share with a general audience.

---

[4] Alma 26:8

[5] I recently had a discussion with my medical provider about a jump in my blood pressure. When I told him I had stopped exercising in the morning in favor of extra scripture study time, he reminded me of the need for balance in all things. I am still trying to find that balance.

[6] See Ether 12:25 (23-29)

[7] See Alma 26:35-37

[8] See 1 Nephi 8:11-12

I will say, though, that I have an indisputable knowledge of the power of God's word to inspire, guide, console, and uplift in matters both big and small.[9]

With few exceptions, this project has been completed with tools that are familiar and widely available to every member of the Church with internet access.[10] I used the print and online versions of the Standard Works and the Church's study helps, such as the Topical Guide. I relied on chance encounters and my memories of recent General Conference talks but did not do an extensive search of the archives with tools like the Scripture Citation Index.[11] I did not consult other doctrinal commentaries or academic research.

By keeping my study methods simple, I hope to highlight the profound power and broad accessibility of God's word by itself. With due respect to scholars who have devoted their lives to understanding the scriptures academically, you do not need the qualifications or resources of a BYU faculty member to have meaningful experiences with the scriptures. You do not need commentaries from others in books and podcasts. (You do not even need to make a spreadsheet or write a book.) These resources can be informative and mind-expanding. They have their place in a gospel studier's library (present work included). It is good to learn with and from others.[12] But it is my testimony that the

---

[9] See Proverbs 3:13

[10] Admittedly, my spreadsheets could not have been developed by everyone, but they could be replicated by anyone with modest skills and a bit of desire. The source data for my spreadsheets is the text of the Book of Mormon, with each verse in its own cell. Everything else in the database is a product of my own study.

[11] This free resource is available on the web at scriptures.byu.edu and as a mobile app named "Scripture Citation Index." It is an index of every scripture reference used in General Conference since 1942, the *Journal of Discourses* (1839-1896), and *Teaching of the Prophet Joseph Smith*. It can also be used to complete advanced text searches of the reference materials.

[12] See Acts 8:26-31

further you get from the source materials—the scriptures and General Conference talks by Church leaders—the more your study will be diluted with the philosophies of men and women. Use other sources, but do not rely on them. A spirit-led study of God's word directly is not only all you *need* to experience the power of God's word, it is the *best* way to motivate tangible, lasting changes in your personal discipleship.

COMING UNTO CHRIST

The most important face of my transformation is an increased conversion to Christ. More broadly, I have come to know each member of the Godhead in ways that I never have before. It is difficult to articulate the significance of that conversion with words, but I have come to a deeper appreciation of the power of sacred music to convey thoughts and feelings that are beyond my power of expression. I quote here a part of a favorite hymn that helps express my feelings, specifically related to my Savior:

> *I marvel that he would descend from his throne divine*
> *To rescue a soul so rebellious and proud as mine,*
> *That he should extend his great love unto such as I,*
> *Sufficient to own, to redeem, and to justify.*
>
> *I think of his hands pierced and bleeding to pay the debt!*
> *Such mercy, such love and devotion can I forget?*
> *No, no, I will praise and adore at the mercy seat,*
> *Until at the glorified throne I kneel at his feet.*
>
> *Oh, it is wonderful, wonderful to me!* [13]

---

[13] "I Stand All Amazed", *Hymns of the Church of Jesus Christ of Latter-Day Saints.* Deseret Book Company, Salt Lake City, Utah. 1985.

Conversion is manifested in improved discipleship. Knowing the Savior better instinctively leads to stronger desires to become like Him. Again, I turn to sacred music to verbalize the feelings of my soul:

> *More holiness give me,*
> *More strivings within,*
> *More patience in suff'ring,*
> *More sorrow for sin,*
> *More faith in my Savior,*
> *More sense of his care,*
> *More joy in his service,*
> *More purpose in prayer.*
>
> *More purity give me,*
> *More strength to o'ercome,*
> *More freedom from earth-stains,*
> *More longing for home.*
> *More fit for the kingdom,*
> *More used would I be,*
> *More blessed and holy—*
> *More, Savior, like thee.*[14]

I have come to imagine discipleship as a large wooden disk with several strings tied around the edges. The disk signifies testimony, and each string represents a religious practice such as scripture study, prayer, Sabbath worship, temple worship, family history work, missionary work, ministering, magnifying callings, etc. When you are intentionally engaged in one of these practices, the string is pulled upward, thus raising that edge of the disk. If you lift the disk with one string, the disk will rotate vertically as you lift, and the string will be in tension with the full weight of the disk. If you pull on two strings, each

---

[14] "More Holliness Give Me", *Hymns of the Church of Jesus Christ of Latter-Day Saints*. Deseret Book Company, Salt Lake City, Utah. 1985.

will have half as much tension, with three strings there will be one third as much tension in each, and so forth. Likewise, each string you add will increase the balance and stability of the disk as you raise it.

At times, it has felt burdensome to add more religious practices to my routine. In the past, I have rationalized my imbalanced discipleship with statements like "I am not much for ministering to others, but at least I am really good at reading my scriptures." I now see that being fully engaged in all gospel practices is not a burden, but a blessing by reducing my reliance on any one practice. The overall weight of nurturing a testimony is the same, but the load is more evenly distributed. There are some practical spiritual safety benefits for taking this approach. If, for whatever reason, something slips in one of my practices, there are others in place to prevent a fall.

None of us can do everything. It is impossible to keep up with every invitation offered by every well-intentioned teacher, speaker, or friend. With King Benjamin, I encourage you to, "See that all these things are done in wisdom and order; for it is not requisite that a man should run faster than he has strength. And again, it is expedient that he should be diligent, that thereby he might win the prize; therefore, all things must be done in order."[15] I am not suggesting you should try to be everything to everyone at every time. What I am suggesting is to take a holistic, balanced, and steadfast approach to your discipleship.

I will not advocate for any one practice being more foundational than any other. They are all important in their own right. The most important thing is to start where you are comfortable. Any improvement in one area will make other improvements feel more instinctive and less burdensome.

For example, I consider myself an introverted person. Scripture study has always come more naturally for me than sharing my testimony spontaneously with an acquaintance or stranger. As I have improved the quality of my scripture study—a place where I was already

---

[15] Mosiah 4:27

comfortable—I have learned the necessity of improving the quality of my prayers as I petition the Lord for His guidance. The combined power of improved scripture study and prayer has led to greater personal revelation and assurance that God knows me, is concerned about me, and has the power to bless my life in the best ways. Like all great experiences, that taste of divine love leaves me with increased confidence[16] and desire to share it with others. Now, when a potential missionary opportunity presents itself, I often surprise myself by opening my mouth and saying something in a way that feels natural and sincere. That is a significant thing for a guy like me.

This is just one example of the many lines I could draw between various religious practices. Part of the magic of my study experience has been seeing more connectivity in the various principles of the gospel than I ever have before. The gospel spiderweb is manifest in the breadth of topics I have written about. I started by studying happiness, but ended up learning about redemption, faith, agency, humility, obedience, discipleship, the plan of salvation, and many other topics. It is that interconnectedness that makes the gospel of Jesus Christ universally accessible and relevant. We all have an easy jumping-off point and much to discover and practice on our journey.

Ammon rhetorically asked, "Who can glory too much in the Lord? Yea, who can say too much of his great power, and of his mercy, and of his long-suffering towards the children of men?"[17] Through this book, I have tried my best to complete Ammon's challenge. However, words can only say so much. Like Ammon, "I cannot say the smallest part which I feel."[18] In short, I have learned to become a truly penitent and humble seeker of happiness.[19] You can too.

---

[16] See Doctrine and Covenants 121:45
[17] Alma 26:16
[18] Ibid
[19] Alma 27:18

APPENDIX A | CITATION INDEX

BOOK OF MORMON

1 Nephi 1:1.................................**114**	1 Nephi 5:21-22 ....**72**
1 Nephi 1:14-16............................ **71**	1 Nephi 5:8 (1-9) **100**
1 Nephi 1:18-20 .... **71**	1 Nephi 5:9 .... **74, 88**
1 Nephi 1:20.................................**88**	1 Nephi 6:4 .... **90**
1 Nephi 1:4, 18 ....**70**	1 Nephi 6:4 (3-6).......................**105**
1 Nephi 1:5-13 ....**70**	1 Nephi 7:1 (1-5) **89**
1 Nephi 1:8, 18-20 ....**54**	1 Nephi 7:12-13 (8-15) **97**
1 Nephi 2:11-13............................ **71**	1 Nephi 7:1-3 ....**75**
1 Nephi 2:12 (12-13) **91**	1 Nephi 7:15 (7, 13-15)............... **96**
1 Nephi 2:14 ....**72**	1 Nephi 7:16................................**75**
1 Nephi 2:1-4...............................**101**	1 Nephi 7:17-18...........................**75**
1 Nephi 2:16 .... **35, 72**	1 Nephi 7:19-21...........................**76**
1 Nephi 2:1-6............................... **71**	1 Nephi 7:20 .... **54**
1 Nephi 2:16 (16-24) **92**	1 Nephi 7:22 .... **76, 88**
1 Nephi 2:17-18 ....**72**	1 Nephi 7:4-5...............................**75**
1 Nephi 2:19-20 (16-24) **100**	1 Nephi 7:6-7...............................**75**
1 Nephi 2:19-24............................**72**	1 Nephi 7:8-15 ....**75**
1 Nephi 2:6-7 ....**88**	1 Nephi 8:1 ....**76**
1 Nephi 2:7................................... **71**	1 Nephi 8:10-13 ....**129**
1 Nephi 3:14 ....**54**	1 Nephi 8:11................................ **137**
1 Nephi 3:19-20............................**72**	1 Nephi 8:11-12 .... **57, 150**
1 Nephi 3:2-4 .... **54, 72**	1 Nephi 8:13 ....**138**
1 Nephi 3:28-30 ....**73**	1 Nephi 8:13,19...........................**130**
1 Nephi 3:31 ....**74**	1 Nephi 8:14, 19-20 ....**139**
1 Nephi 3:7..........................**78, 86**	1 Nephi 8:14-18 ....**129**
1 Nephi 3:8 (5-8) **73**	1 Nephi 8:19-20..........................**129**
1 Nephi 3:9-27..............................**73**	1 Nephi 8:2 (2-34).....................**127**
1 Nephi 4:1-3...............................**101**	1 Nephi 8:21-24, 30 .... **133**
1 Nephi 4:1-4................................**74**	1 Nephi 8:23-24..........................**130**
1 Nephi 4:20-37............................**74**	1 Nephi 8:26-27..........................**139**
1 Nephi 4:6 (4-38) **74, 92**	1 Nephi 8:26-28..........................**130**
1 Nephi 5:1-3................................**54**	1 Nephi 8:30................................**130**
1 Nephi 5:1-8................................**74**	1 Nephi 8:32 ....**139**
1 Nephi 5:21 (10-22) **75**	1 Nephi 8:36-38...........................**76**

Reference	Page
1 Nephi 8:4-10	**129**
1 Nephi 9:1	**76**
1 Nephi 9:6 (2-6)	**102**
1 Nephi 10:13 (12-14)	**101**
1 Nephi 10:17	**127**
1 Nephi 10:19 (15-22)	**29**
1 Nephi 10:22	**29**
1 Nephi 11:1	**127**
1 Nephi 11:21-23	**129**
1 Nephi 11:25	**129, 130, 140**
1 Nephi 11:35-36	**130**
1 Nephi 11:8, 21-23	**57**
1 Nephi 11:8-9	**129**
1 Nephi 11-14	**29**
1 Nephi 11-15	**127**
1 Nephi 12:14-15, 19-23	**101**
1 Nephi 12:16	**139**
1 Nephi 12:1-6	**101**
1 Nephi 13:30-42	**102**
1 Nephi 15:11 (2-11)	**93**
1 Nephi 15:13-16	**102**
1 Nephi 15:2-11	**90**
1 Nephi 15:22	**129**
1 Nephi 15:23-24	**129**
1 Nephi 15:24	**130**
1 Nephi 15:26-27	**139**
1 Nephi 15:26-29	**130**
1 Nephi 15:28	**139**
1 Nephi 15:28-30, 36	**139**
1 Nephi 15:36	**57, 129, 130**
1 Nephi 16:10, 16, 26-30	**77**
1 Nephi 16:18-26, 30-32	**77, 97**
1 Nephi 16:20-25	**54**
1 Nephi 16:28	**80**
1 Nephi 16:28 (26-32)	**93**
1 Nephi 16:32	**88**
1 Nephi 16:34-36	**54**
1 Nephi 16:34-38	**58**
1 Nephi 16:34-39	**77**
1 Nephi 16:4-5 (1-5)	**76, 90**
1 Nephi 16:7	**76**
1 Nephi 16:8	**76**
1 Nephi 16:9 (9-17, 33)	**76**
1 Nephi 17: 23-42, 50-51	**94**
1 Nephi 17:11,16	**79**
1 Nephi 17:13-14	**54, 87**
1 Nephi 17:15	**87**
1 Nephi 17:17-22	**79**
1 Nephi 17:19	**54**
1 Nephi 17:3	**86, 97**
1 Nephi 17:3 (1-3, 12)	**78, 88**
1 Nephi 17:44-55 (23-55)	**79**
1 Nephi 17:5-6	**78**
1 Nephi 17:7-10	**78**
1 Nephi 17:7-18, 49-55	**97**
1 Nephi 18:11	**54**
1 Nephi 18:12-13, 20-22	**93**
1 Nephi 18:1-4	**80, 92**
1 Nephi 18:1-6, 8	**97**
1 Nephi 18:2	**93**
1 Nephi 18:23	**35**
1 Nephi 18:23-25	**81**
1 Nephi 18:5-6, 8	**80**
1 Nephi 18:9-22	**80**
1 Nephi 19:11 (10-17)	**110**
1 Nephi 19:23	**73**
1 Nephi 19:6 (6-7)	**91**
2 Nephi 1:1-5	**90**
2 Nephi 1:17, 21	**54**
2 Nephi 1:21 (16-23)	**52**
2 Nephi 1:24	**54**
2 Nephi 1:30-32	**74**
2 Nephi 1:5, 7 (5-11)	**98**
2 Nephi 2: 15 (11, 15-16)	**133**
2 Nephi 2:1	**54, 112**
2 Nephi 2:10-12	**113**
2 Nephi 2:11	**2, 112**
2 Nephi 2:11 (10-13)	**45, 133**
2 Nephi 2:13	**2, 113**
2 Nephi 2:13 (10-13)	**37**
2 Nephi 2:14	**112**
2 Nephi 2:14 (11-16)	**95**
2 Nephi 2:14-16, 21-24	**113**
2 Nephi 2:15	**133**
2 Nephi 2:23	**45**
2 Nephi 2:24	**45, 108**
2 Nephi 2:25	**45, 112**
2 Nephi 2:25 (17-29)	**108**
2 Nephi 2:27	**39, 112**
2 Nephi 2:28 (26-28)	**141**
2 Nephi 2:7	**113**
2 Nephi 2:8 (3-10)	**114**
2 Nephi 2:8 (3-9)	**125**
2 Nephi 3:1	**55**

2 Nephi 4:17,26 (16-35) **50**	3 Nephi 9:1-12 .... **62**
2 Nephi 4:20 (19-25) **87**	3 Nephi 9:13-14 .... **28**
2 Nephi 4:34-35 .... **103**	3 Nephi 9:13-15 .... **66**
2 Nephi 4:4 .... **98**	3 Nephi 9:13-22 .... **62**
2 Nephi 5:1-7 .... **81**	3 Nephi 9:18 .... **2**
2 Nephi 5:27 .... **31, 35, 81**	3 Nephi 10:1-2 .... **62**
2 Nephi 5:28 (5-28) **35**	3 Nephi 10:3-7 .... **62**
2 Nephi 5:29-33 .... **35**	3 Nephi 10:8 .... **62**
2 Nephi 5:4-26 .... **36**	3 Nephi 10:9-10 .... **63**
2 Nephi 5:6 .... **74**	3 Nephi 11:7 .... **2**
2 Nephi 5:8-19, 27 .... **81**	3 Nephi 11-26 .... **37**
2 Nephi 6:1 (chapters 6-10) **108**	3 Nephi 12:2-12 .... **123**
2 Nephi 7:11 .... **120**	3 Nephi 13: 2, 5, 16 .... **39**
2 Nephi 8:11 .... **67**	3 Nephi 14:15-20 .... **136**
2 Nephi 8:6,11 (3-11) **110**	3 Nephi 14:7 .... **29**
2 Nephi 9:13 (5-26) **112**	3 Nephi 24:14-15 .... **41, 53**
2 Nephi 9:3 (1-4) **105**	3 Nephi 24:14-18 .... **122**
2 Nephi 9:41, 46 (40-46) **112**	3 Nephi 24:16-18 .... **42**
2 Nephi 9:41-43 .... **25, 109**	3 Nephi 27:11 (9-12) **38**
2 Nephi 9:46 (45-46) **122**	3 Nephi 27:32 (30-32) **48**
2 Nephi 9:50-53 .... **144**	3 Nephi 28:4-10, 13-17, 30-31, 37-40 .... **64**
2 Nephi 9:51 .... **43**	
2 Nephi 9:6 .... **112**	3 Nephi 28:5 (1-12) **51**
2 Nephi 11:4-5 (4-8) **114**	4 Nephi 1:15-18 (1-18) **36**
2 Nephi 13:26 .... **120**	4 Nephi 1:16 .... **36**
2 Nephi 15:30 .... **120**	4 Nephi 1:44 .... **64**
2 Nephi 23:8 (4-9) **120**	Alma 3:25-26 .... **60**
2 Nephi 24:3 (1-8) **67**	Alma 3:26 .... **2**
2 Nephi 25:23 .... **98**	Alma 3:26-27 .... **118**
2 Nephi 25:24-27 .... **28**	Alma 4:15 (15-16, 19) **52**
2 Nephi 28:2 .... **106**	Alma 4:2-5 .... **60**
2 Nephi 28:30 .... **94**	Alma 4:6-20 .... **51**
2 Nephi 28:8 .... **38**	Alma 5:26 .... **3, 116**
2 Nephi 30:6 (3-8) **102**	Alma 5:36 (33-42) **120**
2 Nephi 31:17 .... **27**	Alma 5-6 .... **51**
2 Nephi 31:17-20 .... **134**	Alma 7:11-13 .... **65**
2 Nephi 31:3 .... **1**	Alma 7:5 .... **50**
2 Nephi 32:3 .... **144**	Alma 10:13-32 .... **141**
2 Nephi 32:7 .... **55**	Alma 10:5-11 .... **140**
3 Nephi 1:29 (27-30) **48**	Alma 11:21-40 .... **141**
3 Nephi 1:7, 10 (4-13) **56**	Alma 11:34-37 .... **141**
3 Nephi 5:11 (8-11) **105**	Alma 12: 26 (21, 23, 26) **133**
3 Nephi 5:8-10 .... **106**	Alma 12:1-7 .... **141**
3 Nephi 8:20-25 .... **62**	Alma 12:25 .... **117**
3 Nephi 8:23, 25 (19-25) **121**	Alma 12:26 .... **124**
3 Nephi 8:5-19 .... **62**	Alma 12:28-34 .... **125**
3 Nephi 8-10 .... **110**	Alma 16:12-21 .... **37**

Alma 16:20 (15-20)	29
Alma 17:13-18	13
Alma 17:1-4	19
Alma 17:16 (13-17)	125
Alma 17:20	16
Alma 17:20-25	13
Alma 17:2-4	33
Alma 17:26-39	14
Alma 17:5	11
Alma 17:7-12	25
Alma 17:9-11	**23, 34**
Alma 17:9-12	13
Alma 18:2-11	14
Alma 18:22	16
Alma 18:22 (12-23)	14
Alma 18:24-43	14
Alma 18:39 (36-40)	125
Alma 19:11-13	15
Alma 19:14	**9, 15, 51**
Alma 19:1-5	14
Alma 19:16-18, 28-29	55
Alma 19:28-33	15
Alma 19:33-36	15
Alma 19:6	**15, 22**
Alma 20:1-7	15
Alma 20:28-30	16
Alma 20:8-16	17
Alma 20:8-27	16
Alma 21:18-19	16
Alma 21:23 (20-23)	17
Alma 22:1 (1-25)	17
Alma 22:13 (12-14)	125
Alma 22:15	33
Alma 22:25-27	17
Alma 22:3	16
Alma 23:1-6, 18	17
Alma 24:14	126
Alma 24:1-5	17
Alma 24:6-27	18
Alma 25:1-3	18
Alma 25:13-14	18
Alma 25:17	**20, 23, 34**
Alma 26:10	9
Alma 26:11 (1-15)	32
Alma 26:11-16	24
Alma 26:12	2
Alma 26:1-37	20
Alma 26:16	**34, 155**
Alma 26:17	21
Alma 26:17-20	**21, 33**
Alma 26:21-22	**21, 29**
Alma 26:26-35	32
Alma 26:27-30	26
Alma 26:3	22
Alma 26:35	34
Alma 26:35-37	**26, 33, 150**
Alma 26:8	150
Alma 27:1-3	18
Alma 27:16	19
Alma 27:17	**9, 19**
Alma 27:18	**9, 19, 20, 155**
Alma 27:19	19
Alma 27:21-27	37
Alma 27:26 (20-30)	19
Alma 27:4-14	18
Alma 28:11-12	58
Alma 28:12	**61, 111**
Alma 28:14	66
Alma 28:2-6	61
Alma 28:8	**32, 33, 51**
Alma 29:1-2	126
Alma 29:2 (1-3)	66
Alma 30:1-3	61
Alma 30:2	61
Alma 31:24, 30-37	52
Alma 31:5	116
Alma 31:7	115
Alma 32:27 (26-28)	145
Alma 32:28	137
Alma 32:2-8	137
Alma 32:28-34	138
Alma 32:37, 41-43	138
Alma 32:38-40	138
Alma 32:40	137
Alma 32:42	137
Alma 34:15-16	124
Alma 34:16	124
Alma 34:17	28
Alma 34:17 (17-31)	125
Alma 34:31	124
Alma 34:32(31-33)	124
Alma 34:33	40
Alma 34:8-10, 14-15	124
Alma 34:9	123

Alma 35:15-16	**53, 115**	Alma 62:1-2	**50**
Alma 36: 12-14 (6-28)	**20**	Enos 1:10 (9-11)	**120**
Alma 36:15-21	**107**	Enos 1:15-18	**111**
Alma 36-37	**115**	Enos 1:2 (2-8)	**28**
Alma 36-42	**53**	Enos 1:2-12	**111**
Alma 37:1-2, 47	**115**	Enos 1:27	**111**
Alma 37:38-45	**77**	Enos 1:3	**143**
Alma 37:43-45 (38-45)	**93**	Ether 1:1-5	**52, 81**
Alma 37:45	**46**	Ether 1:33	**82**
Alma 38	**115**	Ether 1:34-40	**82**
Alma 39:1-4	**115**	Ether 1:36-37 (33-42)	**90**
Alma 39:16-19	**126**	Ether 1:40-43	**82**
Alma 39:7	**115**	Ether 2:1, 4-5	**83**
Alma 40:1	**117**	Ether 2:10 (7-12)	**82**
Alma 40:12 (11-12)	**122**	Ether 2:13-15	**83**
Alma 40:12 (11-12, 15, 21)	**110**	Ether 2:16 (16-18)	**84**
Alma 40:13-14	**120**	Ether 2:16-19	**93**
Alma 40:15	**2**	Ether 2:19-25	**84**
Alma 40:17	**2**	Ether 2:20-21	**94**
Alma 40:21	**2**	Ether 2:22-25	**94, 98**
Alma 40:23	**118**	Ether 2:6-7	**83**
Alma 41:10-11	**37**	Ether 3:1-6	**94**
Alma 41:2	**118**	Ether 3:1-6, 6:2-3	**84**
Alma 41:2-8	**118**	Ether 3:26-27 (6-28)	**99**
Alma 41:4	**2**	Ether 3:5 (1-6)	**99**
Alma 42:11	**123**	Ether 3:7-26	**84**
Alma 42:12-13	**124**	Ether 6:12	**85, 88**
Alma 42:13 (12-15)	**124**	Ether 6:13	**85**
Alma 42:16-22	**119**	Ether 6:2-3	**94, 99**
Alma 42:22-26	**117**	Ether 6:4	**85**
Alma 42:27-28	**119**	Ether 6:5-11	**85**
Alma 42:29	**20**	Ether 6:17 (17-18)	**85**
Alma 42:31	**125**	Ether 6:9 (5-11)	**89**
Alma 42:4	**132**	Ether 7:27	**56**
Alma 42:5 (4-7)	**124**	Ether 8:1-18	**56**
Alma 42:5-6	**132**	Ether 8:7-10 (1-19)	**58**
Alma 42:8	**124**	Ether 9:1-15	**56**
Alma 42:9 (6-9)	**123**	Ether 9:15	**56**
Alma 44:5	**37**	Ether 11:12-13	**63**
Alma 48:11-13	**19**	Ether 12:15	**20**
Alma 48:17-18	**20**	Ether 12:1-5	**56**
Alma 49:30	**20**	Ether 12:25 (23-29)	**105, 150**
Alma 56:11 (9-11)	**110**	Ether 12:26	**121**
Alma 56:9-11, 17	**53**	Ether 13:2, 15-31	**56**
Alma 59:5-13	**59**	Ether 14:1-31	**56**
Alma 59-61	**50**	Ether 15:1-3	**56**
Alma 60-61	**59**	Ether 15:1-32	**56**

Helaman 3:13-16	**106**	Mosiah 3:19	**20, 137**
Helaman 3:35 (33-35)	**25**	Mosiah 4:1-3, 10-12	**28**
Helaman 6:1-5	**61**	Mosiah 4:26-27	**27**
Helaman 6:20, 37	**61**	Mosiah 4:27	**154**
Helaman 6:33 (26-33)	**48**	Mosiah 5:2 (2-8)	**21**
Helaman 7:1-3	**61**	Mosiah 7:24 (21-26)	**47**
Helaman 7:4-29	**62**	Mosiah 7-22	**47**
Helaman 7:7-9	**61**	Mosiah 8:13-18	**99**
Helaman 9:21-22	**120**	Mosiah 8:8-14	**52**
Helaman 12:1-2 (1-7, 20-26)	**44**	Mosiah 1:16-17	**77**
Helaman 13:38	**37**	Mosiah 2:41	**43, 109**
Helaman 15:2 (1-3)	**121**	Mosiah 16:10-11 (8-12)	**118**
Jacob 1:4 (2-8)	**105**	Mosiah 18:21	**42**
Jacob 2:31 (31-33)	**120**	Mosiah 18:9	**66**
Jacob 4:11	**64**	Mosiah 18:9 (8-11)	**64**
Jacob 4:1-2	**105**	Mosiah 19:26, 28	**59**
Jacob 4:3 (1-4)	**52**	Mosiah 19:29	**59**
Jacob 4:4 (2-6)	**105**	Mosiah 20	**60**
Jacob 6:8	**107**	Mosiah 21:13-16	**60**
Jacob 6:8 (5-11)	**124**	Mosiah 21:2-12	**60**
Jacob 7:26	**31, 55**	Mosiah 21:27	**81**
Jarom 1:2	**111**	Mosiah 21:31-32	**60**
Mormon 1:15 (13-19)	**57**	Mosiah 22	**60**
Mormon 1:2-4	**56**	Mosiah 25:7-12	**50**
Mormon 2:1-2	**57**	Mosiah 26:1-7	**11**
Mormon 2:13 (12-14)	**38**	Mosiah 26:8-13	**11**
Mormon 2:19 (10-19)	**59**	Mosiah 27:11-23	**12**
Mormon 2-6	**57**	Mosiah 27:1-5	**11**
Mormon 3:20-22	**106**	Mosiah 27:24 (24-31)	**12**
Mormon 5:10-11	**63**	Mosiah 27:32-33	**12**
Mormon 5:14 (12-15)	**106**	Mosiah 27:32-37	**12**
Mormon 5:8-9	**48**	Mosiah 27:8	**115**
Mormon 6:17-20 (16-22)	**57**	Mosiah 27:8, 10	**11**
Mormon 6:18 (16- 22)	**121**	Mosiah 27:8-10	**21**
Mormon 7:7 (5-7)	**122**	Mosiah 28:11-12, 17	**81**
Mormon 7:7 (5-8)	**111**	Mosiah 28:1-8	**12**
Mormon 8:38	**2, 39**	Mosiah 28:18 (11-18)	**52**
Mormon 9:14 (11-14)	**119**	Mosiah 28:18 (17-18)	**50**
Mormon 9:2-5	**119**	Mosiah 28:4	**12, 21**
Moroni 2:13	**20**	Omni 1:20	**52**
Moroni 3:3	**28**	Omni 1:21	**56**
Moroni 4:3	**2**	Words of Mormon 1:1-8	**57**
Mosiah 3:13	**28**	Words of Mormon 1:8 (2-8)	**106**

Other Scriptures

1 Corinthians 12:31 .... **30, 121**
1 Corinthians 12:4, 7, 11-12 .... **30**
2 Corinthians 7:10 .... **20**
Abraham 5:10............................. **140**
Abraham 5:8-9........................... **130**
Abraham 5:9 .... **140**
Acts 8:26-31............................... **151**
Bible Dictionary: Exodus, book of **69**
Bible Dictionary: Joshua, book of. **69**
Bible Dictionary: Numbers **69**
  Bible Dictionary: Wilderness of the Exodus **69**
Colossians 1:3-6 .... **135**
Doctrine and Covenants 1:32 .... **28**
Doctrine and Covenants 3:19 (1-3, 16-20) **102**
Doctrine and Covenants 10:66... **143**
Doctrine and Covenants 17:1........ **99**
Doctrine and Covenants 20:77, 79 .... **27**
Doctrine and Covenants 29:35-39 **96**
Doctrine and Covenants 46:11-12. **30**
Doctrine and Covenants 46:30-33 **30**
Doctrine and Covenants 46:8 ...... **30**
Doctrine and Covenants 46:9, 26 **30**
Doctrine and Covenants 52:34... **135**
Doctrine and Covenants 59:23..... **26, 37**
Doctrine and Covenants 63:23.... **141**
Doctrine and Covenants 84:49-53 .... **136**
Doctrine and Covenants 89:18-21 **41**
  Doctrine and Covenants 90:24 (22-24) **26**
Doctrine and Covenants 121:45.. **155**
  Doctrine and Covenants 121:45-46 .... **30**
Doctrine and Covenants 122:7 ... **100**
Doctrine and Covenants 123:12... **141**
Doctrine and Covenants 133:29 (24-35) **142**
Ephesians 2:8-9 .... **98**
Exodus 3:8 .... **86**
Genesis 2:10 (10-14) **140**
Genesis 2:16-17.......................... **131**
Genesis 2:8-9 .... **130**
Genesis 2:9............................ **131, 140**
Genesis 25:29-34........................ **43**
Genesis 3:1-3 .... **131**
Genesis 3:1-5 .... **141**
Genesis 3:22 .... **132**
Genesis 3:23-24......................... **131**
Genesis 3:5 .... **131**
Genesis 3:5-13 .... **131**
Genesis 3:6 .... **133**
Genesis 6:16 .... **94**
Hebrews 5:9 .... **45**
Isaiah 10:15.................................. **22**
Isaiah 14:12-14 (12-17) **96**
Isaiah 35:6-7 (1-10) **142**
Isaiah 40:31............................... **100**
Isaiah 5:20 .... **41**
Isaiah 53:2-5 (2-12)..................... **65**
Isaiah 55:1 .... **142**
Isaiah 55:2-13............................ **144**
Isaiah 57:15 (15-21) **39**
Isaiah 63:7-10.............................. **66**
James 4:3 (3, 6-8) **30**
James 4:8-10 .... **20**
Job 34:35 .... **146**
John 1:12-17 .... **98**
John 1:1-3, 12-14 .... **136**
John 1:14 (1-4, 14) **65**
John 4: 10, 14 (5-26) **141**
John 7:37-38.............................. **141**
John 11:35, 38 (1-44) **66**
John 15:1-11 .... **98**
Lamentations 1:4-6 .... **120**
Lamentations 2:8-11................... **120**
Luke 6:45 (43-45) **27**
Luke 8:12................................... **136**
Luke 8:13................................... **136**
Luke 8:14................................... **137**
Luke 8:15................................... **137**
Luke 12:29-34.............................. **27**
Malachi 3:10-12 .... **42**
Malachi 3:14-15 .... **53**
Mark 7:16 .... **128**

Matthew 5:3-12	**123**
Matthew 5:45	**53**
Matthew 6:19-20 (19-33)	**43**
Matthew 6:19-21	**27**
Matthew 6:33 (31-34)	**26**
Matthew 7:15-20	**136**
Matthew 10:38-39	**63**
Matthew 11:28-29	**43**
Matthew 11:28-30	**66**
Matthew 12:33	**136**
Matthew 13:19	**136**
Matthew 13:20-21	**136**
Matthew 13:22	**137**
Matthew 13:23	**137**
Matthew 13:4	**136**
Matthew 13:5-6	**136**
Matthew 13:7	**136**
Matthew 13:8	**136**
Matthew 16:24-25	**63**
Matthew 26:1-5	**141**
Moses 1:39	**96**
Moses 3:10 (10-14)	**140**
Moses 3:16-17	**131**
Moses 3:8-9	**130**
Moses 3:9	**131**, **140**
Moses 4:11, 28	**131**
Moses 4:11-19, 22-25, 29	**131**
Moses 4:28	**132**
Moses 4:29-31	**131**
Moses 4:3(1-4)	**96**
Moses 4:7-9	**131**
Moses 5:10-11	**45**
Moses 7:18	**63**
Moses 7:28 (23-40)	**66**
Philippians 4:13	**98**
Philippians 4:7	**95**
Proverbs 3:13	**151**
Proverbs 3:5	**86**
Proverbs 11:30	**130**
Proverbs 14:34	**37**
Psalm 23:4	**46**
Revelation 2:7, 22:14	**130**
Revelation 7:14-17 (9-17)	**142**
Revelation 21:5-6	**143**
Revelation 22:2 (1-3)	**130**
Romans 8:28	**95**

General Conference

Dale G. Renlund, "Latter-day Saints Keep on Trying"	**109**
David A. Bednar, "And Nothing Shall Offend Them"	**96**
Dieter F. Uchtdorf, "Happiness, your Heritage"	**148**
Dieter F. Uchtdorf, "Yearning for Home"	**128**
Neil L. Andersen, "Spiritually Defining Memories"	**90**
Robert D. Hales, "Waiting upon the Lord: Thy Will Be Done"	**100**
Russell M. Nelson, "Hear Him"	**110**
Russell M. Nelson, "Joy and Spiritual Survival"	**40**
Russell M. Nelson, "Revelation for the Church, Revelation for Our Lives"	**91**, **95**
Russell M. Nelson, "We Can Do Better and Be Better"	**113**, **135**

MISCELLANEOUS

"Tree of Life", music by Mack Wilberg, text by David Warner **128**
American Dictionary of the English Language **10, 32, 142**
American Society of Civil Engineers (ASCE) Code of Ethics **6**
C. Wilfred Griggs, "The Tree of Life in Ancient Cultures" **127**
    Camille West, "New Tree of Life App Lets You Explore and Teach Lehi's Vision"
....**128**
Gospel Topics **41**
History, 1838–1856, volume C-1 .... **107**
Hymns, No. 131 .... **153**
Hymns, No. 193 .... **3, 7, 152**
Hymns, No. 30 .... **69**
Hymns, No. 86 .... **3**
Mark Staker, "Tree of Life: Lehi's Dream—A Shared Vision" **128**
Saints, Volume 1, The Standard of Truth **69**
Saints, Volume 2, No Unhallowed Hand **69**
Scripture Citation Index **151**
Strong's Exhaustive Concordance of the Bible **142**
The Family: A Proclamation to the World **41**

APPENDIX B | BOOK OF MORMON VERSE COUNT TIMELINE

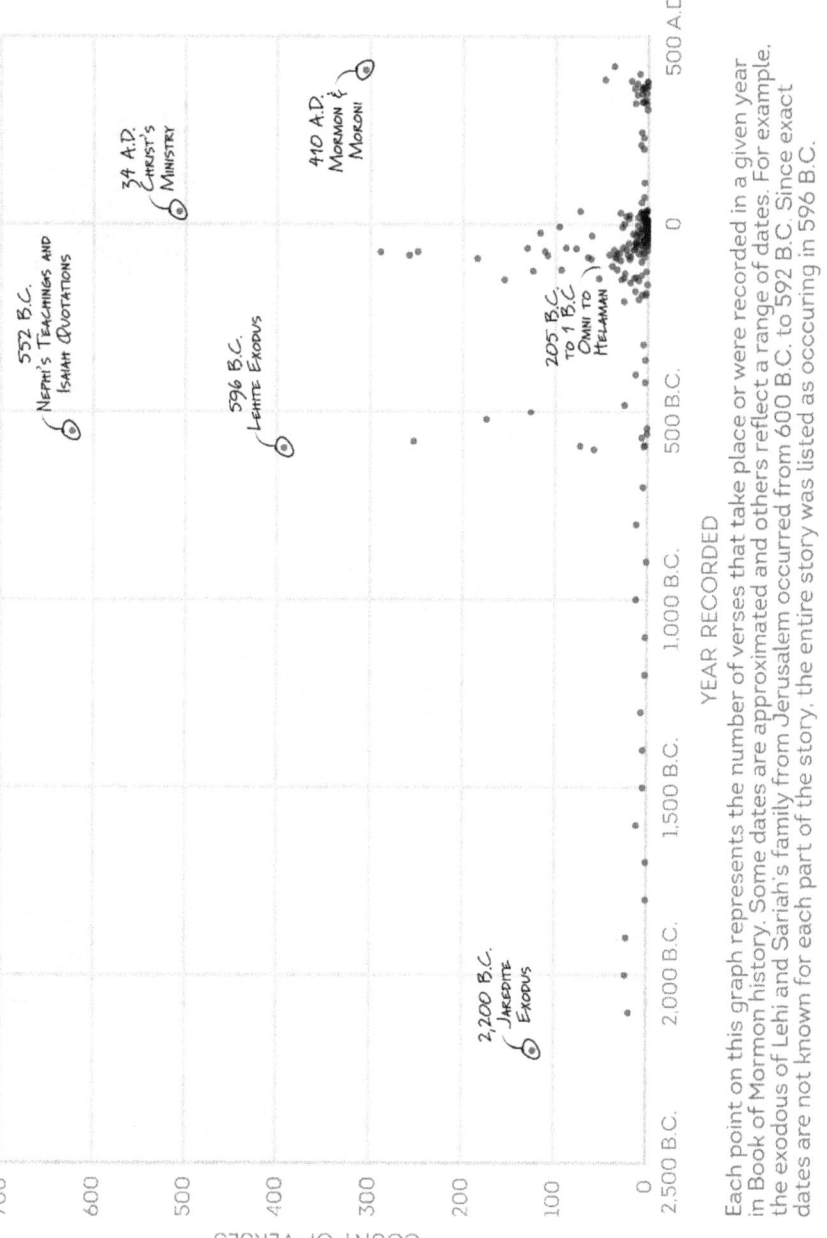

About The Author

Dane has a family, house, job, church calling, and a deep love of the scriptures. He wrote this book not because it was a natural outgrowth of his professional credentials, but because he needed to study the topic for his own benefit. As he deliberately studied happiness from the Book of Mormon, he learned things that were too good to not share with others, and so *The Humble Seeker of Happiness* was born. He intentionally chose the title, not only because it hints at a prominent theme, but because it succinctly summarizes his own faith journey.

Dane holds a master's degree in civil engineering from Utah State University and works full time as an airport engineering consultant. Originally from Blanding, Utah, he now seeks happiness with his wife, Danielle, and their three children in Utah's beautiful Cache Valley.

Printed in the USA
CPSIA information can be obtained
at www.ICGtesting.com
LVHW041403310124
770461LV00073B/2480